Reason To Write

WRITING FOR THE GED AND BEYOND

Bird Stasz   Matthew Adams   Maryanne Felter

CAMBRIDGE ADULT EDUCATION
A Division of Simon & Schuster
Upper Saddle River, New Jersey

To Meghan, Jeffrey, Jack, Jane, Rebekkah, and Chris
May you grow to think clearly, speak truthfully, act wisely,
and may you leave the world a little better place for your passing.
With love, Bird, Maryanne, and Uncle Matt

Executive Editor: Mark Moscowitz
Project Editor: Renée E. Beach
Editor: Roberta Moore
Production Director: Penny Gibson
Production Editor: Rosann Bar
Production: Pencil Point Studio
Art Direction: Joan Jacobus
Marketing Manager: William Jarred

Copyright © 1996 by CAMBRIDGE ADULT EDUCATION, a division of Simon and Schuster, One Lake Street, Upper Saddle River, New Jersey 07458. All rights reserved. No part of this book may be reproduced or transmitted in any form or by any means, electrical, including photocopying, recording, or by an information storage retrieval system, without permission in writing from the publisher.

ISBN: 0-130-83602-8
BA8

10 9 8 7 6 5 4 3 2 1   99 98 97 96

CAMBRIDGE ADULT EDUCATION
A Division of Simon & Schuster
Upper Saddle River, New Jersey

Acknowledgements

There is not a book in the world that does not owe its heart to many people other than the authors and this one is no exception. Collectively, we owe an enormous debt of gratitude to Douglas O. Michael and his incredibly competent staff at the Cayuga Community College Library. Not only did they help us solve research questions, but they maintained a sense of humor when we did not. We also need to thank Shirley Kunkel who listened to pieces and parts of this manuscript, who maintained a sense of equilibrium when we occupied her printer for hours at a time, and who was always encouraging and cheerful. To Sandra S. Kelley we owe a significant note of thanks for being willing to try out many of these exercises in her classes. We thank, too, Greg Szczepanski, who worked out every computer glitch and made it possible for us to beam this book back and forth across the miles through cyberspace. A note of sincere appreciation goes to Dr. Daniel Schultz who opened his thirty-year collection of interesting and thoughtful material and who was endlessly patient no matter how many questions or interruptions came his way. We simply could not have written this book without him. To our students at Wells College and Cayuga Community College, especially Mandy and Lillian, who patiently tried everything, critiqued carefully, and wrote volumes, thanks. Matt owes special thanks to his friends who loaned him their computers so he could work on this thing. Thanks to Nelle Gregory, Myles Presler, and Todd Steinwart.

Finally, we thank Mark Moscowitz whose incredible patience and tenacity kept us going through writing and revision.

Contents

Why This Book?	vi

CHAPTER ONE
RISK AND RESPONSIBILITY — 1

Chapter Goals	1
Introduction	1
Values: Are You What You Believe?	2
The Story of Sammy Snipes	3
Exercise 1.1: Values Clarification	4
Prewriting Strategies	5
Freewriting	5
Exercise 1.2: Focused Freewrites	6
Writing Tips	6
Brainstorming	6
Exercise 1.3: Brainstorming Practice	7
Classification	8
Exercise 1.4: Looking Inward	9
Exercise 1.5: Looking Outward	9
Definition	10
Exercise 1.6: Defining Your Terms	11
Case Study 1: *Linda Riss v. City of New York*	12
Exercise 1.7: Group Discussion and Reflection	13
Mapping	14
Exercise 1.8: Idea Map	14
Writing Strategies	15
Summary Writing	15
Exercise 1.9: Summarizing	15
Journalists' Questions	16
Exercise 1.10: Answering Journalists' Questions	16
Summary/Response Writing	17
Exercise 1.11: Annotating Your Reading	17
Writing Topic Sentences	17
Exercise 1.12: Writing Topic Sentences	18
Facts, Assumptions, and Opinions	18
Exercise 1.13: Fact, Assumption, or Opinion?	19
Exercise 1.14: Supporting Opinions with Facts	20
Finding a Fact Pattern: Compare and Contrast	21
Case Study 2: *Kline v. 1500 Massachusetts Avenue Apartment Corporation et. al.*	22

Exercise 1.15: Comparing Fact Patterns	23
Exercise 1.16: Contrasting Fact-Pattern Exercise	24
More Risk and Responsibility Cases	25
Case Study 3: *Farwell v. Keaton*	25
Exercise 1.17: Defining Responsible Behavior	26
Case Study 4: *Myrrhic Waters, et. al. v. Timothy Blackshear*	27
Exercise 1.18: Reviewing a Court's Decision	27
Chapter Review: Putting It All Together	28
General Writing Topics	29
Extra Writing Practice: Quotation Notation	29

CHAPTER TWO
PARENTING, FAMILIES, AND CHILDREN — 30

Chapter Goals	30
Introduction	30
Values: Familial, Cultural, and Regional	31
Exercise 2.1: What Do You Think?	32
Exercise 2.2: Values, TV, and Your Thinking	32
Isms, Biases, Stereotypes	33
Exercise 2.3: Free Your Mind	34
Essays: Not Just for Tests	35
Elements of a Good Essay	35
Exercise 2.4: The Thesis Statement	36
Good Essay Form	36
Exercise 2.5: Mark It Up	38
Compare and Contrast Essays	39
Essay Topic: Child Support	41
Case Study 1: *Edith Maude Hendry v. Joe B. Hendry, Jr.*	41
Exercise 2.6: Essay Practice	42
Case Study 2: *Tammy Lynne Hernandez v. Miguel Carlos Hernandez*	42
Exercise 2.7: Compare and Contrast Essay	43
Metaphors, Similes, Analogies	45
Exercise 2.8: Writing Analogies	46
Exercise 2.9: Extra Essay Practice	46
Chapter Review: Putting It All Together	47
General Writing Topics	48
Extra Writing Practice: Quotation Notation	48

CHAPTER THREE
PRIVACY, CONFIDENTIALITY, AND THE RIGHT TO KNOW — 49

Chapter Goals	49
Introduction	49
Values: Are You How You Behave?	50
Exercise 3.1: Valuing Privacy	51
Cause and Effect	52
Causal Relationships	52
Exercise 3.2: Finding Causal Relationships	52
Causal Connections	54
Case Study 1: *Griswold v. The United States*	55
Exercise 3.3: Finding Causal Connections	56
Cause-and-Effect Essays	56
Exercise 3.4: Essay Practice	58
Exercise 3.5: The Importance of Feedback	58
Media and the Right to Privacy	59
Case Study 2: *Sidis v. F-R Publishing Corporation*	59
Exercise 3.6: Group Reflection and Discussion	61
Cause and Effect: So What?	61
Exercise 3.7: Cause/Effect Evaluation	61
Exercise 3.8: More Essay Practice	62
Developing Your Ideas with Details	63
Exercise 3.9: Detail Practice	63
Exercise 3.10: Revision Practice	64
Essay Topic: Individuals and the Right to Privacy	65
Case Study 3 (Part 1): *Judith Ann Harkey and Jeanne R. Harkey v. Michel Abate*	65
Exercise 3.11: Reflection and Discussion	66
Case Study 3 (Part 2): *Harkey and Harkey v. Abate*	66
Exercise 3.12: Cause-and-Effect Essay	66
Case Study 4: *Richard M. Ribas v. Joan Clark*	67
Exercise 3.13: Cause-and-Effect Essay	67
Case Study 5: *Time, Inc. v. James J. Hill*	68
Exercise 3.14: Reflection and Discussion	69
Exercise 3.15: Cause-and-Effect Essay	69
Chapter Review: Putting It All Together	70
General Writing Topics	70
Extra Writing Practice: Quotation Notations	71

CHAPTER FOUR
CIVIL RIGHTS AND THE CONSTITUTION — 72

- Chapter Goals — 72
- Introduction — 72
- Rights: Are They Guaranteed? — 73
    - Exercise 4.1: The Rights "Quiz" — 73
    - Exercise 4.2: Making Civil Rights Your Rights — 74
- Revise and Reflect — 75
- Essay Topic: Civil Rights: A Historical Perspective — 75
    - Exercise 4.3: Essay Practice — 76
- Argumentation — 77
- EATO in Action — 78
    - Exercise 4.4: Essay Practice — 78
- Essay Topic: Gender and the Constitution — 79
    - Exercise 4.5: Outlining Arguments — 79
- Structuring an Argument — 80
    - Exercise 4.6: Structuring Arguments — 81
    - Exercise 4.7: Essay Practice — 85
- Extended Analogies — 85
    - Exercise 4.8: Reflection and Discussion — 87
- Case Study 1: *Fred Toyosaburo Korematsu v. United States* — 87
    - Exercise 4.9: Reflection and Discussion — 90
    - Exercise 4.10: Essay Practice — 90
- Argumentative Context — 90
    - Exercise 4.11: Shifting Context — 91
    - Exercise 4.12: Essay Practice — 91
- Fallacies in Argument — 92
- Types of Fallacies — 93
    - Exercise 4.13: Fallacy Practice — 93
    - Exercise 4.14: More Fallacy Practice — 95
- Essay Topic: Freedom of Speech — 95
- Case Study 2: *Bethel School District No. 403 v. Framer* — 95
    - Exercise 4.15: Argumentative Essay — 96
    - Exercise 4.16: Argumentative Essay — 96
- Case Study 3: Freedom to Cheer — 97
    - Exercise 4.17: Argumentative Essay — 97
- Chapter Review: Putting It All Together — 98
- General Writing Topics — 98
    - Extra Writing Practice: Quotation Notations — 99

ANSWER KEY — 101

Why This Book?

There is much that is right about the world in which we live, and there is much that could stand some fixing. What we fix, what we celebrate, what we build, and what we take down can rest on the information we receive and how we process that information. We live in what many have called the "information age": never before has there been so much data, so many stories, tidbits, and theories transmitted from one place to another. With this data overload, who knows what becomes a critical piece of information? Furthermore, as those of us with great access to information are constantly being persuaded, convinced, and kept informed, we may become almost numb to the events and circumstances of the world that are brought to us every day.

With so much overload, it is often very difficult to weed through the onslaught and find the information that is significant to our lives and our communities. In writing this book, it is our hope that we can help people take a strong step in organizing, reflecting, and creating information that is relevant to themselves, their communities, and their cultures.

Conflict, confusion, and prejudice can be, at least in part, credited to how information is processed. This book will ask you, its reader, to reflect critically on your own beliefs and assumptions as well as the arguments, beliefs, and assumptions that are presented to you. In this book there are very few "answers." Rather, this is a book of questions.

It is also a book about writing your ideas down with a certain degree of commitment and power. The process of writing is also the process of thinking. For some, writing about ideas is the best way to clarify and solidify thinking. By the same token, sharing one's writing and learning to write well are powerful tools at a person's disposal. They allow an individual access to the greater discussions of family, community, and government.

At the least, getting together with people and challenging each other's views and writings is fun; at its most, it is liberating.

What is This Book?

This book is divided into four chapters or units, each with a general theme that focuses on cultural and political beliefs and positions. They are risk and responsibility, family, privacy/the right to know, and civil rights. Each chapter has real court cases that relate directly to the topic. The cases represent the problems and challenges of ordinary people dealing with real issues—sometimes in extraordinary ways. In a broader sense, these cases examine how, from a legal standpoint, American culture views contemporary issues. We have also included excerpts from some of the Supreme Court decisions because they are examples of fine writing. (None of us is a lawyer, though. The legal discussions in this book should not be considered in any way to be legal advice.) Each chapter has a section called

"Quotation Notations." We hope that these quotations, which are relevant to the topic(s), spark some discussion and thought. Our students in our workshops have enjoyed the opportunity to think about and work with quotations, and we hope you do the same. Throughout each chapter, there are many exercises on writing, thinking, problem solving, and constructing arguments. It is not necessary to do every single exercise, but we would urge you to work from the beginning of the book to the end as each chapter builds on the one before. Select what works for you, and go for it.

Paragraphs: A Review

Most of the writing exercises in this book are focused around the essay. The backbone of the essay is the paragraph because essays are composed of a number of paragraphs. Our students in our workshops often find it helpful to review what a paragraph is before they take on bigger and more complicated writing challenges. Therefore, we suggest that you review the basic concept of paragraphs and do some of the exercises before you start.

    A paragraph is a set of related sentences about one particular topic. For example, a paragraph about tulips would not include much information about zinnias. A paragraph almost always includes a topic sentence. A topic sentence focuses for the reader what the paragraph is about. It is also the most general statement in the paragraph. To continue with our tulip example, a good topic sentence might be, *Tulips are one of the most popular spring flowers.* Following a topic sentence, you will find sentences that flesh it out. These sentences can do many things: they might define the topic, might give examples of the topic, or might explore the topic in some other way. But each sentence in the paragraph will be about the main topic of the paragraph. No sentence will bring in another topic. If you want to discuss another topic, start a new paragraph. Finally, a paragraph has to make sense. It needs an organizational framework that helps the reader understand what you are trying to say. Organization comes in many ways and depends a great deal on what you, the writer, want the paragraph to do. For example, if you are writing a paragraph about making tacos, then you will probably organize the paragraph in order as to what to do first, second, and so forth. If you are writing a paragraph about an abstract idea such as love or greed, you might want to organize it around a definition of the term. No matter what you write, organization is key. Keep it in mind as you work on these paragraph exercises.

Paragraph Practice

Below are two paragraphs. Locate the topic sentences and the supporting information. We have modeled one for you.

Example: Tulips are one of the most popular spring flowers. (Topic sentence) Their popularity exists because *they are so easy to grow and look wonderful after the long hard winter. Tulips come in many varieties and colors,* which adds to their popularity. *One of the most versatile flowers of the garden,* tulips have been popular for years.

1. I hate winter because life becomes so complicated. It is always cold. You have to wear tons of clothes and boots, so even going outdoors takes on new problems. The roads are covered in snow and are usually slippery. It takes forever to get to work. The house is never warm enough, and the heating bill grows each month. We have to cut cords of firewood. Every time a log comes into the house, there is dirt and wood chips all over the floor. Cleaning takes up most of my time. There is little doubt that winter can't end soon enough to please me.

2. Computers are a blessing and a curse for writers. Computers allow writers to zip along, writing like the wind. Ideas just flow onto the page without a thought to spelling and grammar. Computers make revisions a breeze. Computers also are cranky and ill tempered. Some writers believe that the computer has an evil elf that lives inside the microchips just waiting to make life miserable. This usually occurs when the writer loses a day's worth of work and doesn't have a copy because of some weird computer malfunction. There is little doubt that writers can't live without computers and can't live with them.

Exercise 2

Below you will find topic sentences. Choose one or two, and write paragraphs to go with them. Exchange them with others in your class to get feedback on your work.
1. Basketball is a great spectator sport.
2. Chocolate is one of the great luxuries of life.
3. Learning to write well is (easy, hard, fun, frustrating).
4. Reading to children is important because it helps them do better in school.
5. Telling lies will most likely get you into big trouble.

Paragraph checklist:
1. Do you have a topic sentence?
2. Do all of your sentences relate in some concrete way to the topic sentence?
3. Does the paragraph make sense, that is, is it organized in such a way that a reader can follow easily what you are trying to say?

We hope that this little review session was helpful. You are probably ready to move on into the rest of the book by now. We urge you to have fun and enjoy writing.

CHAPTER One

RISK AND RESPONSIBILITY

Chapter Goals
After studying this chapter, you will be able to:
- Use prewriting strategies, such as freewriting, brainstorming, and classifying.
- Understand the importance of defining terms and clarifying ideas in your writing.
- Extract important information from written material and summarize it.
- Separate facts from assumptions and opinions, and use facts to support your ideas when you write.
- Compare and contrast information to identify fact patterns and draw conclusions.

Introduction

If little Andre leaves his blocks on the front steps of his apartment building and Mrs. Jones trips on one and breaks her hip, can she sue Andre's parents? If you see a thug harassing a child, should you do something about it? If you walk down a deserted street late at night, should you expect to be mugged? Who is at fault if you do get mugged? Questions like these highlight the ideas of **risk** and **responsibility** in our society.

What people are and are not responsible for has, in many ways, become a legal rather than a moral question. In fact, the notion of risk and responsibility as legal issues has changed our lives. People who act with poor judgment causing someone else to suffer may be found legally liable for negligence. **Liable** is another way of saying "responsible." **Negligent** is another way of saying "careless." The greater the risk a person takes, the greater his or her responsibility for the outcome. For example, a few winters ago in Colorado, a group of four cross-country skiers set off on a trek during a snowstorm. Two of the party were experienced skiers, and two were not. During the course of the day, the snowstorm became a blizzard, and the group was separated. The two experienced skiers made it to safety and sent the mountain rescue team to search for their friends. It all ended well with everyone safe. However, the volunteer rescue team sued the skiers for negligence because the team felt that they were needlessly put at risk. The experienced skiers made a very bad judgment call that could have had fatal results. This is an example of risk, responsibility, and the law.

This chapter will give you an opportunity to think about risk and responsibility, not only from a legal point of view, but also as moral and ethical issues. You will have a chance to explore some interesting ideas while reading and reflecting on actual legal cases. Some of the outcomes in these cases are downright scary. These selections were made on purpose to provoke you into thinking hard and writing clearly.

Values: Are You What You Believe?

As you read further, you will discover that your ideas about risk and responsibility stem from your values. **Values** are powerful ideas that shape people's lives. If you ask the soldier on the battlefield why he or she is fighting, the answer will probably involve the values of country, God, and bravery. If you ask Mother Teresa why she devoted her life to the poor of India, she would speak of her devotion to her faith. If you ask the Wall Street millionaire why he or she amassed so much money, the response would likely have something to do with the thrill of the game and the value of wealth. A person's values influence the way that person sees the world and ultimately behaves. Some would say, in fact, that you are what you believe. The tricky thing about values is that we are not always clear about what we believe.

Being clear about beliefs is especially important when you write about or argue about a topic. If you aren't really clear about what you believe about an issue and where that belief comes from, it becomes tough to support your point of view. As a result, you can wind up making arguments that seem logical on the surface but really are not. Being clear about what you believe and why also helps you to understand the other side(s) of an argument. The ability to separate values from facts and to be able to see both sides of a question is key to becoming a good writer, a good thinker, and finally a good citizen.

The following story presents a situation that will help you to think about and identify your own values.

The Story of Sammy Snipes

Sammy S., also known as Sammy the Actor, was one of America's truly great bank robbers. Born in Brooklyn as the son of a blacksmith, Sammy left school early and began his career as a shoplifter and small time thief. By the 1920s, he had apprenticed himself to Doctor Dan, who was one of the foremost safe-crackers in the United States. Doc taught Sammy everything he knew.

By the 1950s, Sammy's career was moving along well. He fell in love, was married, and continued to rob banks. Unfortunately, he became so well known that he had to move out of his house and go underground. He took a handyman's job at a residential nursing home that provided him room and board. He was so "hot" that he could not even see his wife and baby daughter.

George M., the police commissioner of the New York Police Department, was a rising star in police circles. He was making a name for himself and his department by capturing criminals. Commissioner M. was often seen on the front page of *The New York Times* as he arrested one underworld figure after another. He decided that the best way to catch Sammy was to put out a wanted poster with his picture and offer a large reward.

Arnie S. was a 24-year-old clerk in his father's dry-goods store in Brooklyn. Being a very ambitious young man, Arnie was always looking for a quick way to make money. On his way home from work one chilly fall day, he was waiting for the subway, when much to his surprise, he spotted Sammy S. Arnie seized the opportunity for fame and fortune. He found a police officer on the corner and told him that Sammy S. was on the train. The police officer quickly arrested the famous bank robber.

Arnie went home to choose a new suit for the reward ceremony. Unfortunately, the police commissioner held a commendation ceremony for the arresting officers and forgot to invite Arnie. He also forgot about the $70,000 reward. The next day Arnie, his dreams of wealth evaporating before his very eyes, hired an attorney to sue the city so that he could receive the $70,000 reward for the tip. Arnie's lawyer reminded the commissioner of his obligations, and in no time Arnie S. was a wealthy man. His picture was on the front page of *The New York Times,* and he was booked for radio and TV appearances. He described himself as a "model citizen, only doing his job."

Soon after, Arnie S. was murdered on his way home from work. This had nothing to do with Sammy S. despite Sammy's underworld connections. Arnie S's father, Big Lou S., in a state of extreme grief, decided that the only sensible thing to do was to sue the city for pain and suffering because his son did not receive adequate protection from the NYPD. Commissioner M. raised a $25,000 reward for Arnie's killer. He also appeared on the front page of *The New York Times* as often as possible to show his commitment to fighting crime.

Exercise 1.1: Values Clarification

1. Rank the characters in the story from most offensive to least offensive with 1 being the most offensive and 5 being the least offensive. Then write a sentence or two explaining your answer.

   a. _____ Sammy S.   d. _____ Arnie S.
   b. _____ Doctor Dan   e. _____ Big Lou S.
   c. _____ George M.

2. Get together with others in your class, and compare and discuss your answers. Using the information from your discussions, make a values list that shows what the group values and believes.

   Example:

   Five people thought that Sammy S. was the worst because he was a crook and broke the law all the time.

   Ten people thought that Big Lou S. was the worst because he did not seem to care about his son's death—all he wanted was money.

   Six people thought that Arnie S. was the worst because all he cared about was money and himself.

   Two people thought that the commissioner was the worst because he was only interested in his career when he was supposed to care about the public.

3. Use your group values list to write a short piece on the types of values that people today seem to hold, as represented by your class. What, for example, if nine-tenths of the class picked one character as the worst and no one picked another character? What does that say about how the people around you feel about certain values?

   Example:

   Our society values money and power too much. It seems that everyone is out to make as much money as they can anyway that they can. Even public servants, whose job it is to protect people and who are paid by taxpayers, seem to care only about getting ahead. We talk a great deal about doing good things for people and our community but when it comes down to it, most people don't really think about others at all.

Prewriting Strategies

Have you ever sat down to write and found that you had nothing to say? The pressure is on: you have an essay due at 8 A.M. the next morning, and you know that you have to produce something. Unfortunately, as the pressure builds, so too does the **writer's block**—the inability to put words on the blank page. **Prewriting strategies** can help you release the ideas in your mind and overcome writer's block.

In the following section, there are four prewriting strategies for you to try:

1. Freewriting
2. Brainstorming
3. Classifying
4. Defining

Later, you may elect to use all or some of these strategies as you write.

Freewriting

Quite simply, freewriting helps you get ideas on paper. Here's how it works.

1. Get a blank sheet of paper and a pen or pencil or, if you have one, a computer.
2. Set a timer for ten minutes. (Ten minutes is not a rigid rule. You can freewrite for as long as you want, but ten minutes is a good "average" amount of time.)
3. Start your timer and start to write. Do NOT stop for any reason until the timer rings.
4. NEVER look back. Don't reread what you've written. Don't stop and think. Just keep writing.

There are no rules in freewriting. You can misspell, leave out punctuation, write fragments—all of those things you've been told NOT to do for years. The point is not to worry about the form but to get the ideas out of your head as quickly as you can. The only rule is that you must never stop writing. If you find yourself stuck with nothing to say, continue to scribble on the paper or to write things like, "I'm stuck I have nothing to say what can I say now I really don't know what I'm doing oh Lord this is awful this is weird this is whatever." Eventually, your mind will become unstuck and return to the topic again. You may get off the topic; just try to force yourself back on. Anything goes in freewriting. No one but yourself will ever read it. It is yours and yours alone.

You can do "open" freewrites on any subject or thing or emotion that comes to your mind. This can be good practice. However, writing on a particular theme or subject helps you to draw out your ideas. This is called **"focused" freewriting.**

Exercise 1.2:   Focused Freewrites

Write for ten minutes on one of these topics.
1. The riskiest thing you ever did
2. A good lesson you learned about responsibility
3. What makes a good parent
4. A big mistake you made
5. A skill you have
6. What makes a good friend
7. Someone you admire
8. The type of job you want

Writing Tips

1. When you've finished your freewrite, go back and read what you've written.
2. Cross out the scribbles and everything that gets off the topic. That makes it easier later to find information you're looking for.

Brainstorming

Most of us do a fair amount of brainstorming. If you're a person who makes yourself lists of what you have to do, you **brainstorm** all the time. When you brainstorm, you let all your ideas on a topic flow freely. Brainstorming is a prewriting strategy, and it works especially well as a follow-up exercise after freewriting. To brainstorm, examine one of your freewriting pieces (especially focused freewrites), pick out your main points, and put them in a list. Read your list a few times; any time a word or idea sparks a new idea or word, add it to the list. Often, you will come up with some things that you did not cover in your freewriting. There is nothing magical or dramatic about any of this, but it can be a helpful way to get your ideas on paper. The only rule in brainstorming is that everything goes. There are no right or wrong answers.

Example:
Topic: Responsibilities of Parents to Their Children
1. provide basic needs such as

   | a place to live | clothes | food | warmth |
   | safety | health care | discipline | love |

2. be a good role model
3. help them learn right from wrong
4. make sure they go to school and do their homework

5. help them learn responsibility
6. help them to stay out of trouble
7. help them think about and plan their future

Exercise 1.3: Brainstorming Practice

1. Brainstorm on any one of the topics below.
   a. Responsibilities of schools to students
   b. Responsibilities of parents to children
   c. Responsibilities of families to their members
   d. Responsibilities of employers to employees
   e. Responsibilities of elected officials to the people who elected them
   f. Responsibilities of school boards to the community
   g. Responsibilities of a minister, rabbi, or priest to his/her parishioners
   h. Responsibilities of a doctor to his/her patients
2. Once you have a list, write a paragraph or two about the topic.

Example:

Responsibilities of Parents to Their Children.

One of the biggest responsibilities of parents is to make sure their children have the basic things they need to grow up. They need a place to live that is safe and enough food so that they can grow right. They need to eat good food, not just junk. Children need a warm place to live and decent clothes to wear. They don't need fancy shoes that cost one hundred dollars, but they do need to look nice so that their friends will give them respect. Parents also need to make sure they keep their children healthy and take them to the doctor or clinic when they need to go.

Children need more than the basics from their parents. They need to have parents whom they can look up to and who teach them about right and wrong. Parents are supposed to see to it that their children go to school and do their homework. When children are in trouble the parents should help them understand how not to make the same mistake again. Parents have the big responsibility of helping children think about the future and plan for it. That may mean getting a good education or learning a skill or trade. But most of all, the biggest responsibility is that parents give their children the love and guidance that they need to grow up to be strong and become good parents to their own children when the time comes.

Classification

Another way to focus your thinking about an idea is to look at it as an exercise in classifying. **Classifying** means placing ideas, people, events, and other things into categories. Classification is one of the most natural ways that humans deal with new information and situations. In fact, it is one of the first thinking strategies that children develop. For example, when a child first learns that his pet is a dog, the child begins to point to every animal from a giraffe to a llama and say "doggie." What the child is doing is working out the ingredients, characteristics or elements of doggieness and placing "dog" in a larger category called "animals." The child is trying to figure out what makes a dog a dog and why a giraffe is not a dog. Eventually, the child learns to classify different types of animals, as well as the elements that go into making up "doggieness," because everyone agrees on what a dog is and is not.

The process that we go through as children to work out the classification of concrete things is the same process that we use to classify abstract ideas and concepts. There are two parts to this process. The first is *looking inward* to determine the elements or characteristics of an object or idea. The second is *looking outward* to see what applications or variations of that object or idea there are. To return to the dog, the inward elements of the classification of *dog* are such things as four legs, fur, domesticated, common pet, carnivorous, and descended from the wolf. The outward elements of the classification can be summed up in breeds such as wolfhounds, labradors, poodles, and mutts; or in functions such as seeing-eye dog, hunting dog, and guard dog.

The hardest part of classifying ideas and concepts is that much of the inward and outward looking is **subjective**; that is, it depends on the person. For example, if you are a fabulous swimmer, you might not classify jumping into a swimming pool as something risky. If you can't swim, however, jumping into a pool is very risky.

Exercise 1.4: Looking Inward

1. In the list below, check off what you think are the ingredients, or elements, of risk. Keep in mind that for a classification to work, it must have broad application (the outward look). (There are no *right* answers.)

   a. ____ fear
   b. ____ loss
   c. ____ big gains
   d. ____ big responsibility
   e. ____ authority
   f. ____ reputation
   g. ____ luck or chance
   h. ____ no prior planning
   i. ____ a gamble
   j. ____ peril
   k. ____ change
   l. ____ stability
   m. ____ safety
   n. ____ future
   o. ____ unknown
   p. ____ known

2. Compare your list to others in the class. As a group, make a list of "risk" elements that all can agree on; feel free to add to the list.

Exercise 1.5: Looking Outward

1. Below are some applications of risk. Rank order them from 1 to 5 with 1 being the most risky and 5 the least risky.

   a. ____ Going out on a blind date with someone you met through an ad in the paper
   b. ____ Giving up a job that pays well for one that pays better but that requires you to move somewhere you hate
   c. ____ Becoming involved with someone who is married
   d. ____ Delivering a package with unknown contents from a stranger
   e. ____ Leaving your children with a male baby-sitter

2. Now add five applications on your own. Try not to make your statements too obvious.

   a. _____
   b. _____
   c. _____
   d. _____
   e. _____

3. Go back to your group and exchange statements with a partner. Rank the partner's risky statements, just as you did above. Now, as a group, try to answer the following questions:
   a. Does everyone in your group agree that all the statements in #2 are examples of risk? If not, which ones are not examples of risk and why not?

b. What do all the group members' statements that are high risk have in common?

c. What do all the statements that are considered low risk have in common?

4. From your discussions, write a paragraph or two concerning what you or your group believe to be true about the "classification" risk. Include thoughts from your explorations of the "inward look" at risk, as well as the "outward look" at risk.

Example:

Our group felt that what made a situation risky was easy to understand when the risks were big but harder to understand when the risks were not so big or obvious. We all agreed that if someone were going to be physically harmed, that was definitely a risk. We also agreed that if someone were going to lose a lot, that was definitely a risk. We agreed that the "unknown" and "fear" are a big part of what makes something a risk. We discovered that deciding whether something was risky really depended on the individual person and her experiences except in the obvious cases. We also agreed that there are all kinds of risks, some more challenging than others.

Definition

What you may have just discovered in the previous exercise is that thinking and talking about ideas like risk is more complicated than it looks. You begin to see how many different understandings of an idea there can be and how those differences can cause confusion. It is important, therefore, when you write that you get used to the idea of defining your terms—if not on the page, at least for yourself.

There are two parts to a definition. The first is **denotation,** or what the word literally means as defined in the dictionary. For example, here is the literal definition of the word *risk* from *The American Heritage Dictionary of the English Language:*

risk (n) 1. The possibility of suffering harm or loss; danger. 2. A factor, element, or course involving uncertain danger; hazard.... tr.v. risked, risking, risks. 1. to expose to a chance of loss or damage or hazard: "I had seen him risk his limbs blindly at the fox-hunt" 2. to incur the risk of: His action risked a sharp reprisal

The second part is connotation. **Connotations** are meanings of the word that will not show up in the dictionary but that the word carries with it. Although not all words have connotations, when they do, the connotations are more difficult to get hold of. For example, some words, such as *mother-in-law*, have a specific denotative meaning (mother of a person's spouse) but carry many connotative meanings as well: an interfering, obnoxious, whining person whom one cannot get rid of short of divorce. *Librarians* are people who work in libraries, but the term has picked up the connotations of bookish, boring, out of touch with reality, and petty. The word *responsibility* may have connotations for some people as well: some people see it as burdensome, a thing that takes all the spontaneity out of life, something to be avoided as long as possible. *Risk* is seen by some as something exciting, a way of living on the edge and bringing thrills to their lives. Others associate risk with fear and dread and a collapse of order.

If you look at how words work in different situations, you will come to see how connotations can change, depending on who uses the word and when it is used. It is these connotations that make clear communication challenging. By concentrating on what *you* mean by a word before you use the word, you can clarify ideas in your head as well as on paper. Also, by being aware of the connotations and denotations words have, you will be able to use words more precisely in your writing, thereby communicating more clearly.

Exercise 1.6: Defining Your Terms

1. Practice writing definitions of concrete ideas. Define each word below as you think it might be defined in a dictionary.

   Example:
   Ice hockey: a game played by teams on ice skates, using sticks to try to score by getting the puck into the other team's goal.

   a. Football: _____
   b. Apartment: _____
   c. Garden: _____
   d. Milkshake: _____

2. Now try to write what you think is a pretty good definition of the word responsibility.
   _____
   _____

3. Get into a group of three, and read each other's definitions. See if you can find common agreement. Combine the three definitions into one. Look carefully at what you have written. Have you embedded in your definition any connotations of which you may not have been aware at first? Denotative definitions are objective; be sure yours is.

4. Share all the group definitions with the class. Are they similar? Are there elements of some definitions that you would like to incorporate in your own group's definition? Check your group definition with the dictionary. How close are you?

CASE STUDY 1:
Linda Riss v. City of New York

Linda Riss, a 23-year-old secretary, became involved with Burton N. Pugach. Pugach, 32, who was an attorney living in Scarsdale, a wealthy community outside of New York City. Many of its residents are successful professionals who work in Manhattan. Mr. Pugach was no exception.

Pugach and Riss established a romantic relationship that was going along quite well until Riss discovered that Pugach was married. Riss at that time decided to end the relationship.

Pugach, however, continued to contact Riss. His calls became insistent and finally turned vicious. He repeatedly threatened to have Riss killed or maimed if she did not yield to him. It was reported that he even went so far as to tell her, "If I can't have you, no one else will have you, and when I get through with you, no one else will want you."

Riss, in fear for her life, contacted the New York City Police department in February. They established that Riss was a "reputable woman," but they did not offer her any protection. During the remainder of the year, Riss repeatedly contacted the police department with additional pleas for help. Other witnesses verified that Riss's safety and well being were at risk as Pugach continued to threaten her. During one of her many interviews with the NYPD, a detective told Riss that unless Pugach actually hurt her, the police could do nothing for her.

A few months later Riss met another man. Their engagement was announced at a party in the couple's honor on June 14. The next morning, Heard Harden was driven by Al Smith to Riss's apartment in the Bronx. Harden, posing as a delivery man with an engagement gift, convinced Riss to open her door. When she did, he hurled a bottle of lye into her face. Riss was blinded in one eye and lost a good portion of her vision in the other; her face was permanently scarred. After the assault, the NYPD concluded that Miss Riss was indeed in danger and provided a policewoman as round-the-clock protection for the next three-and-one-half years. When Pugach was arrested, the police found a revolver in his briefcase. He was charged with violation of the Sullivan law (possession of a handgun). Also arrested were three men, Harden, Luis, and Newkirk, who had allegedly been hired by Pugach to attack Riss. Harden, Luis, and Newkirk were all convicted and sent to jail.

Riss sued the New York City Police Department for negligence for their refusal to provide her with protection after her repeated requests. Her suit went up to the New York State Court of Appeals and was not upheld. The basis of the majority opinion revolves around two questions.

The first is, "What is the responsibility or duty of a municipality (in this case New York City) toward its citizens?" The majority opinion held that the police department is charged with providing protection from external hazards and controlling the activities of criminals. The City of New York provides resources to the police department and is responsible for determining how they get their job done. The court cannot "proclaim a new and general duty of protection"—which means that it cannot tell the police department how those resources can be spent.

The second question concerns professional judgment, specifically, who decides who should be protected from what? The court is reluctant to play "armchair quarterback" and to judge cases on the basis of hindsight. The thinking of the court is that a police officer must be able to exercise professional judgment when responding to a crisis. According to the majority opinion, because the NYPD is responsible for the safety of citizens in general, it is not responsible for the safety of any one individual in particular. Therefore, if Riss won this suit, it would set a new standard of operations for branches of the government like police departments and would open the floodgates for law suits.

Exercise 1.7: Group Discussion and Reflection

Asking good questions is at the very heart of learning to think critically and to write critically. Think about the following questions, and discuss them in a group.

1. Would there have been less of a responsibility on the part of the city if Riss had been attacked after the first threat rather than after repeated threats?
2. For three-and-one-half years after the incident, Riss was given round-the-clock protection. Didn't the city show good faith in doing this?
3. Does the government have a responsibility to make sure that individuals live in personal security? Why or why not?
4. If so, does the government have a responsibility to get rid of dangerous living conditions, such as slums, crack houses, street gangs, and drug dealers, all of which are a danger to the lives of citizens?
5. Does the fact that Riss's "reputable personality" was established affect your response to her situation? If she had been a "disreputable person," would the police have acted any differently?
6. What *is* a "reputable personality" anyway?
7. Can you think of similar situations in which people were left at risk and, in fact, hurt because of an organization's failure to provide adequate protection?

Mapping

Lawyers involved in the Linda Riss case made two opposing arguments. One side argued that Linda Riss was at risk and the police department did not do its job protecting her. The other side disagreed. Like most cases, the argument is not black and white; neither side is clearly right nor clearly wrong. Rather, the argument takes on "shades of gray." Therefore, in constructing an argument, it is important to organize your thoughts carefully.

Mapping is one way to organize your thoughts. Mapping is a way of showing graphically the connections between ideas. In mapping, you take an idea, a word, or a phrase, write it in the center of the page, and circle it. Draw ideas, words, or phrases that come from this as off-shoots from the main idea. These secondary ideas often suggest more words and ideas, and these, too, are drawn in. The process keeps going until you are out of ideas. Often, people find themselves inspired by one particular strand of ideas, and they spend time developing this strand. These strands and maps can act as outlines for organized writing as you start your central point and move down the map into details and supporting ideas and thoughts.

Example:

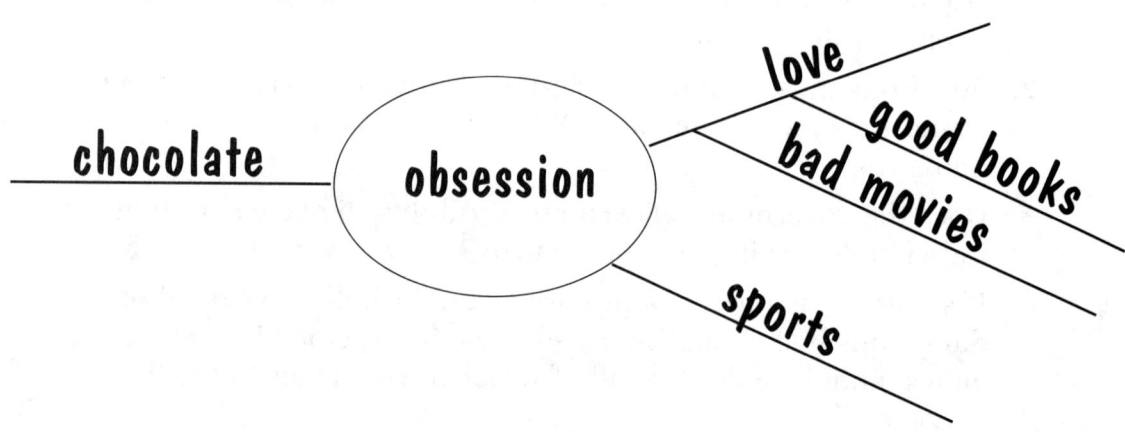

Exercise 1.8: Idea Map

Map the Riss case. Place an idea (for example, police protection) in the middle of the circle. This exercise is easier done with a partner. There are no right or wrong answers. If you are having trouble remembering what actually happened, go back and review the case again.

Writing Strategies

At this point, you are ready to use prewriting strategies to develop written pieces. You will begin by using the Riss Case to develop your ideas about risk and responsibility.

First, you will try several writing strategies based on extracting information from the case. These strategies are:

1. Summary writing
2. Asking journalists' questions
3. Summary/Response writing

Later, you will read more cases and develop longer pieces using these strategies:

4. Writing topic sentences
5. Identifying facts, assumptions, and opinions
6. Using fact patterns to compare and contrast information from different sources

As you do the writing exercises throughout this section, you are encouraged to work with a partner or in a group to develop ideas and edit each other's work.

Summary Writing

Now it's time to try some writing. One of the most useful things to learn how to write is a summary. A **summary** boils down all the information that you have into a concise piece. Summaries are more than just shorter versions of longer works. A summary must include the most important information organized in a way that makes the most sense to the reader.

To summarize, read the text a few times, noting carefully the key information. Underline anything you think is essential.

Exercise 1.9: Summarizing

1. Underline all the facts in the Riss case.

    Example:

    Linda Riss, a 23-year-old secretary, became involved with Burton N. Pugach. Pugach, 32, was an attorney living in Scarsdale, a wealthy community outside of New York City. Many of its residents are successful professionals who work in Manhattan. Mr. Pugach was no exception.

    Linda Riss, a secretary, became romantically involved with Burton Pugach, an attorney in wealthy Scarsdale, New York.

2. Go back through the case paragraph by paragraph, extracting the highlighted information, and write a summary of the entire case. It might help you to look back at your map to be sure that you have covered all of the important points.

3. After you have written your summary, switch papers with a partner and compare. Do you both have the same information? Now, compare your summary with the example below:

Example:

Linda Riss, a secretary from New York City, was the victim of her ex-boyfriend's revenge and the object of police neglect. Linda Riss was disfigured and partially blinded because she refused to see her ex-boyfriend Pugach, an attorney from Scarsdale. After Riss broke off their relationship because she found out that Pugach was married, he continued to stalk her and to make threatening phone calls. Riss went to the police on many occasions, asking for their help and protection. In every instance, she was refused until one day Pugach sent a hired "hitman" to throw acid on her face. After the attack, the NYPD provided Riss with round-the-clock protection. Linda Riss sued the NYPD for negligence. Her case went all the way to the top court in New York.

Journalists' Questions

Another way to get the ideas to develop a summary is to use **journalists' questions** (who? what? when? where? why? and how?). Journalists' questions are particularly effective if you are writing a factual summary such as the one you have been working on.

Exercise 1.10: Answering Journalists' Questions

Example:

Who? Linda Riss, Pugach, and the NYPD

What? Woman attacked and disfigured despite asking for police protection

1. Fill in the rest of the answers.
   When? _____
   Why? _____
   How? _____

2. Rewrite your summary, using the above journalists' questions as a way of organizing your writing. Is your summary any different from the first one you wrote, if so how?

Summary/Response Writing

Most of the time, you will not be writing summaries. Most writing assignments ask you to react, usually to some source you have read. Reacting is always easier once you know exactly what the source says—therefore, the summary writing. Often, before you can react to a source in writing, you need to tell your audience what that source was about—again, summary. But the most important part of summary/response writing is the response—what YOU think about what the source says. **Summary/response** writing asks you to report someone else's story, idea, or position and to explain what your opinion about it is. Once again, marking the original text is helpful.

Exercise 1.11: Annotating Your Reading

1. Reread the Riss case, making notations in the margins. Your notations should include reactions to the text, questions about the text, and any comments you have or connections you can make to your own life.

2. Review your marginal annotations, and extract your opinions from the other comments you have made. List or circle your opinions. Then write a one- or two-paragraph statement on your opinions about the case.

Writing Topic Sentences

An important element of good writing is the topic sentence. A **topic sentence** tells the main idea of the paragraph and prepares the reader for what is to come. Writing topic sentences can help you clarify your own thinking and focus on a particular point. There are some easy rules to make writing topic sentences easy:

1. The topic sentence is the most general sentence in the paragraph.
2. The topic sentence tells the reader two things: what the topic of the paragraph is and what your slant on that topic is.
3. The topic sentence can appear at the beginning, middle, or end of a paragraph. Usually, it is best to place it at the beginning.
4. The topic sentence answers, "What do you want the reader to remember?" or "What are you really trying to say?"
5. If you put all the topic sentences in an essay together, they will form the skeleton of a summary.

Exercise 1.12: Writing Topic Sentences

Write a topic sentence for each of the following topics.

Example:

TOPIC:
The responsibility of parents to children

TOPIC SENTENCE:
A parent's responsibility to his or her children involves caring for physical needs as well as psychological, moral, and sociological development.

TOPIC:
The risks involved in changing a job

TOPIC SENTENCE:
A job change involves financial, familial, and psychological risks.

1. **TOPIC:** *The responsibilities of a student*
   TOPIC SENTENCE: _____
   _____

2. **TOPIC:** *The responsibilities of a police department*
   TOPIC SENTENCE: _____
   _____

3. **TOPIC:** *The risks of traveling alone*
   TOPIC SENTENCE: _____
   _____

4. **TOPIC:** *The risks of caring for children*
   TOPIC SENTENCE: _____
   _____

Check your topic sentences to be sure that they identify the topic and give your opinion about the topic.

Facts, Assumptions, and Opinions

In the late 1960s, a magazine published two photographs of the same person hitchhiking. It posed the question, "Which man would you give a ride to?" In the first picture, the young man wore a pair of dress slacks, a tie, and a blazer; he had short, neatly-styled hair. In the other photograph, the young man wore torn jeans and a T-shirt, his hair was very long, and he carried a guitar and a backpack.

Overwhelmingly, readers responded that they would give a ride to the first young man but not the second. What happened? The person didn't change at all, just his appearance. As his appearance changed, so did the assumptions of the onlookers. Assumptions are powerful things and can easily be confused with facts.

A **fact** is something that can be proven and on which almost everyone would agree. An **assumption** is something that you believe to be true but which cannot necessarily be proven. Some assumptions turn out to be facts, but others do not.

Assumptions often require you to draw a conclusion that may or may not be correct. For example, in the Riss case Linda made the assumption that the police would protect her because she believed that was their job. She also assumed that the person knocking on her door was really a delivery man.

To return to the hitchhiker example, you might assume that the well-dressed young man is an all around nice guy and is "safe." In fact, he may be an escaped axe murderer. You may assume that the greasy "hippie" with the guitar is "on drugs" and would be a real danger to you. In fact, he could be a really nice, independently wealthy person who wants to share his fortune with the world.

An **opinion** is a strongly held belief that may or may not be based on personal knowledge or facts. For example, a person may say, "In my opinion, so and so should get a job," or "She is a rotten person," or "Everyone who belongs to that club is a snob." These are statements of opinion that may be based on facts or on assumptions. The problem with facts, assumptions, and opinions is that they are often used interchangeably in arguments and discussions, which causes all sorts of problems. Therefore, it is important for writers and thinkers to understand the difference and to be able to hunt down the assumptions and opinions behind an argument as well as the facts that support the argument.

Exercise 1.13: Fact, Assumption, or Opinion?

In the list below, identify the facts, assumptions and opinions.
(F = Fact; A = Assumption; O = Opinion)

_____ 1. Levi jeans are made in the United States.

_____ 2. People from cold climates believe that Hawaii is paradise.

_____ 3. A red sunrise in the Rockies in December means snow.

_____ 4. A group of young men walking down the street at night is dangerous.

_____ 5. If you break the law, you will be punished.

_____ 6. Women make better single parents than men.

_____ 7. Chopping down the rainforest will eventually affect our climate.

_____ 8. Native Americans have a right to their own land.

_____ 9. Standardized test scores in mathematics are declining nationwide.

_____ 10. The invasion of Grenada was a good idea.

_____ 11. The Persian Gulf War was necessary.

_____ 12. *Brown v. the Board of Education of Topeka Kansas* marks the legal beginning of school desegregation.

Exercise 1.14: Supporting Opinions with Facts

Below you will find a summary/response of the Riss case written by a student. The writer uses facts to support her opinion, and she also makes certain assumptions about her subject. Read through the piece carefully, and list all the facts, assumptions, and opinions used in the paragraph.

> *The courts in New York State were wrong to find that the New York City Police Department was not negligent in its failure to protect Linda Riss from her one-time lover, now attacker, Burton Pugach. I believe that it is the duty of police departments to protect their citizens, and the New York City police failed to protect Riss. Riss was a secretary. She could hardly protect herself from him either at work or in her private life. When Pugach started to harass her, she complained to the police, but they said they could do nothing to help her. In fact, the police said that until Pugach actually DID something to her, there was nothing they could do. But this is ridiculous. It means that if someone threatens your life, it's OK. It's only not OK if the person kills you. But by then it's too late, isn't it? If the police department had done something right away when Riss complained, Riss would not have been blinded. So really the police were to blame for Linda Riss' misfortune.*

After you think you have sorted out the facts, assumptions, and opinions, get together in a small group and compare answers. Then see if your results match the results below. The facts are underlined, the opinions are italicized, and the assumptions are capitalized.

> *The courts in New York State were wrong to find that the New York City Police Department was not negligent in its failure to protect Linda Riss from her one-time lover, not attacker, Burton Pugach. I believe it is the duty of police departments to protect their citizens,* and the New York City police failed to protect Riss. Riss was Pugach's secretary. *SHE COULD HARDLY PROTECT HERSELF FROM HIM EITHER AT WORK OR IN HER PRIVATE LIFE.* When Pugach started to harass her, she complained to the police, but they said they could do nothing to help her. In fact, they said that until

<u>Pugach actually did something to her, there was nothing they could do</u>. *But this is ridiculous. It means that if someone threatens your life, it's OK. It's only not OK if that person kills you.* <u>But by then it's too late, isn't it?</u> IF THE POLICE DEPARTMENT HAD DONE SOMETHING RIGHT AWAY WHEN RISS COMPLAINED, RISS WOULD NOT HAVE BEEN BLINDED. *So really the police were to blame for Linda Riss' misfortune.*

Your results may or may not match the sample. What you will notice, however, is that there is very little fact used in this paragraph. For an opinion to be truly convincing, it needs to be supported by as many facts as possible. So although this paragraph does put forth an opinion and attempts to argue it, it presents a fairly weak defense of its opinion. This is why it is so important to learn to distinguish between facts, assumptions, and opinions. Therefore, in the next section, you will continue to work on fact finding.

Finding a Fact Pattern: Compare and Contrast

In the course of your studies as well as in your work life, you will have to read material from different sources and sort out information. For example, if you decide to buy a new car, it would be silly to drive into the first lot and buy the first car you see. It would make more sense to look at newspaper ads, visit several dealerships, talk with your friends, and read a magazine such as *Consumer Reports*. When you make your purchase, it will be an informed decision based on a collection of facts.

You can use this same process to construct and write arguments. In the legal profession, this is called establishing a **fact pattern.** Lawyers use this method to analyze their present case; look at similar cases; sort out facts, assumptions, and opinions, and draw up an argument or conclusion.

To find fact patterns, you need to sort the similarities and differences found in different sources. When you compare facts, you show how they are similar. When you contrast facts, you show how they are different. Understanding how to develop a fact pattern will help you use information more effectively in your writing. In the process, you will also become a better reader.

To practice this technique, consider two cases: *Riss v. City of New York*, which you have already read, and *Kline v. 1500 Massachusetts Avenue Apartment Corporation et. al.*, which follows. (You may want to go back and reread the Riss case to refresh your memory.)

CASE STUDY 2:

Kline v. 1500 Massachusetts Avenue Apartment Corporation et. al.

Sarah Kline rented an apartment in a 585-unit apartment complex in Boston, Massachusetts. The main entrance of the apartment complex was located on Massachusetts Avenue, with side entrances on both 15th and 16th Streets. A full-time doorman was on duty at the main entrance, and a desk clerk was assigned 24 hours a day to the elevators in the lobby. The 15th Street doorway was connected to a parking garage which, at the time Kline signed the lease, had two attendants on duty at all times. The 16th Street entrance was left unattended during the day but was locked by 9 P.M. every evening. Kline chose this complex to live in because of its central location and good security.

Seven years later, the main entrance had no doorman, and the desk in the lobby was left unattended much of the time. The garage personnel had been laid off, leaving the garage entrance unattended, and the 16th Street entrance wasn't locked at night. During the same period of time, crime in the neighborhood was rising. To quote Kline, "You couldn't help but notice the police cars around the building."

Kline, as well as other tenants in the complex, spoke repeatedly to the landlord about their concerns for security. The record shows that there were 20 police reports of crimes occurring in the building in one year. There were several occasions when female tenants woke up to find strangers breaking through their front doors. At one point, muggings and burglaries were reported to occur on a daily basis.

When Kline was mugged and robbed by a male intruder in the hallway outside her second-floor apartment, she sued the owner of the apartment complex. Kline won her suit. The court held that the landlord had been given notice that the tenants were in danger from criminals and was aware that crimes against the tenants were likely to continue. Furthermore, the landlord was providing security when the tenants became residents and, therefore, set a personal "standard of care." The court held that the landlord was under a "duty of protection" and was liable for Kline's injuries.

To establish a fact pattern, look for facts and ideas that are common to both the cases. Pay attention only to those things that are significant by being central to the case, general in nature, and applicable to other situations. For example, in the Kline case the fact that Kline lived in Boston is not significant, but the fact that Boston is a large urban area is. The fact that Linda Riss lived in the Bronx, specifically, isn't significant either. The fact that she lived in a city, however, would be part of your fact pattern because the Bronx and Boston are both urban areas. *"City"* and *"urban"* are general ideas, not specifics. Because both Riss and Kline were women living in urban areas, these ideas would, therefore, be included in your fact pattern. These are significant ideas, they are key to the material, they are general in nature; and you could find similar cases that have those ingredients.

Exercise 1.15: Comparing Fact Patterns

1. Develop a fact pattern comparing the Kline and Riss cases. Both cases involve:

    a. women

    b. living in an urban area

    c. victims of violence

    Complete the list, using the following questions to guide you.
    - Who did they ask for protection?
    - What happened when they did?
    - Why did they think they could ask for protection in the first place?
    - What happened to the protectors?
    - What was similar about their environments?

    d. _____

    e. _____

    f. _____

    g. _____

    h. _____

    Look back over your fact pattern and make sure that you have included only similarities. Are any of the things on your list really differences?

2. Review your fact pattern with a partner. Then, write a paragraph that talks about the similarities between the two cases. Be sure to begin with a topic sentence that explains that you are talking about similarities and tells the reader that you are dealing with the Kline and Riss Cases. (In other words, be sure you write a topic sentence that both identifies the topic and establishes your slant on that topic.)

3. Switch papers with another partner. Answer the following questions about his or her paragraphs.

    a. Does the topic sentence use the word similarities?

    b. Does the topic sentence mention the names of Kline and Riss?

    c. Does the paragraph include all of the facts in the fact pattern?

    d. Does the paragraph make use of specific details from the cases?

    e. Did the writer draw any conclusions that do not seem to make sense? If so, what are they?

    f. What did you like best about the paragraph?

    g. What do you want to know more about?

    h. What ideas do you have to help the writer improve the paragraph?

4. Read the sample paragraph below. Apply the above questions to this paragraph. Then, based on your answers to the questions, try to improve the paragraph by rewriting and expanding it.

    Kline and Riss both lived in an atmosphere of urban unrest. They were both victims of violent crimes while they had depended on others for security. That betrayal was further intensified when after asking the local police departments for help, they received little assistance. Although their cases were similar, the results of those cases were quite different.

Exercise 1.16: Contrasting Fact-Pattern Exercise

Write a paragraph which shows how the Kline and Riss cases are significantly different. You will find that the differences are not nearly as obvious or as easily explained as the similarities.

More Risk and Responsibility Cases

Following are more cases that show how the issues of risk and responsibility are interpreted by the law. Each one shows a slightly different view of what responsibility is and what constitutes a risk. The cases have different outcomes; they are also quite different from the two you have already worked on, Riss and Kline. The purpose of including more cases is to give you a chance to consider the concepts of risk and responsibility from different points of view.

CASE STUDY 3:

Farwell v. Keaton

On the evening of August 26, 1966, David Siegrest, age 16, and Richard Farwell, age 18, drove to a trailer rental lot to return an automobile that Siegrest had borrowed from a friend who worked there. Siegrest and Farwell planned to wait in the car until the friend had finished work and then "drive around," stopping at various restaurants and drive-ins. While they were waiting for the friend to finish work, Siegrest and Farwell drank about four or five beers each.

Shortly before nine o'clock, two teenage girls walked by the entrance to the lot. The two boys tried to engage them in conversation. Both boys left the car and followed the girls down the street to a drive-in restaurant.

The girls complained to their friends in the restaurant that they were being followed. Six boys left the restaurant and chased Siegrest and Farwell back to the rental lot. Siegrest got away unharmed by ducking into the trailer rental office. He asked those inside to help his friend, but by then Farwell had been caught by the group and severely beaten. He was found hiding underneath his car in the rental lot.

Farwell went to the trailer office, where Siegrest gave him a plastic bag of ice for his injuries. Between ten and midnight, the two boys drove around visiting at least four other drive-in restaurants. Farwell said that he was tired and wanted to lie down so he climbed into the back seat of the car. Around midnight, Siegrest drove the car to the home of Farwell's grandparents, parked it in the driveway, and tried to wake up his friend. When Farwell couldn't be woken and made only a little sound as if in a deep sleep, Siegrest left him there and went home himself. The next morning, Farwell's grandparents found him and took him to the hospital, where he died three days later from an epidural hematoma, a severe bruising of the brain.

Farwell's father brought suit against Siegrest for "breach of his legal duty to use reasonable care after coming to the aid of [his friend], and that such negligence was the proximate cause of the decedent's death."

Translation: According to the suit, Siegrest, in helping his friend, had a responsibility to get Farwell medical attention or, at the very least, to notify someone of his injury and where he was.

Roughly speaking, the idea of legal negligence questions the way individuals behave in certain situations. In short, responsible action is judged by a common standard of behavior. The difficult notion here is that the idea of "responsible behavior" is hard to define.

The case brings up the question: "What is the legal responsibility of friendship?" In this case, negligence (carelessness) occurred because Siegrest did not provide enough, and the right kind of, help to his friend. As a result, his friend died of an injury that, if treated right away, has an 85 percent survival rate. The other part of this case is that the two boys were social companions "engaged in a common undertaking" where one person knew that the other had been injured and could have helped him without harm to himself but did not act in a "reasonable" way.

Exercise 1.17: Defining Responsible Behavior

Write several paragraphs that answer some of the following questions. You may want to work with a partner.

1. Without focusing solely on the legal points, what do you think about this case?
2. What is your responsibility to your friends when you go out?
3. What kinds of effects could a case like this one have on social behavior?

This chapter has discussed the nature of risk and responsibility as they are interpreted by the law. In Riss, the issues of risk and responsibility revolved around personal safety and police responsibility to provide protection. In Kline, risk and responsibility had to do with rights of tenants and the responsibility had to do with rights of tenants and the responsibility of landlords. In the above case, risk and responsibility are entwined with personal friendship and appropriate action. In this next case, risk and responsibility are involved in a legal discussion of the consequences of a children's prank.

CASE STUDY 4:

Myrrhic Waters, et. al. v. Timothy Blackshear

On June 6, 1987, Timothy Blackshear, approximately 10 years old, was playing with firecrackers with his friend Myrrhic Waters who was 7. Timothy was lighting the firecrackers, tossing them on the ground, and watching them spin. After about ten minutes of doing this, he placed a firecracker in Myrrhic's sneaker. Myrrhic was unaware of the firecracker and was burned. Myrrhic and his mother sought recovery of damages, suing Timothy solely on the theory that he was negligent. The judge told the jury that the Waters could only "recover damages" if Timothy's actions were not intentional and were negligent.

The underlying idea here is that negligent conduct cannot be deemed legally negligent if it is intentional.

As you can see when you read this case, definitions become very important. For example, Timothy could be held "liable" for battery because he intentionally put a firecracker in Myrrhic's shoe and lit it. But he could not be found liable for "negligent conduct." So the question is, "What exactly is negligence?" Battery has a specific definition: "The unlawful application of force to the person of another resulting in grievous bodily injury."

Exercise 1.18: Reviewing a Court's Decision

Write several paragraphs that respond to the following questions. You may want to work with a partner.

1. Should children be sued?
2. Should a 10-year-old be charged with battery?
3. What are the long-term consequences of actions such as these?
4. Should cases like this one even come to court?
5. What are some other arguments you could make about this case?
6. How do these court decisions affect the lives of us all?

CHAPTER REVIEW
Putting It All Together

Think back over all four of the cases you have read, and write a fact pattern that includes ALL of them. Make a list of the similarities among all the cases by looking carefully at the facts of each case.

Before you start, let's review the different techniques you might use to help you pull all of this information together.

1. Freewrite and see what comes out; perhaps you will find that you have already made some connections among the cases in your mind.

2. Use journalists' questions to locate the who, what, why, where, when and how of each case, focusing on the basic facts and establishing quickly a review of each case.

3. Reread each case and underline all the facts, making comments and notations in the margins of each case.

4. Use mapping (this is best done in a small group or as a class) so that you can see graphically what the facts of each case are.

5. Try all of the above.

Once you have established the fact pattern of the cases, look carefully at your information, and make sure you have identified similarities among the general ideas just as you did in the fact pattern for Riss and Kline. Be sure you are talking not about specifics, but about underlying principles that these cases seem to have in common.

If you have done this carefully and thoroughly, you will have the basis for quite a good essay on the topics of responsibility and risk. Write several paragraphs that discuss your opinion of a particular aspect of risk and responsibility based on the cases you have read. Be sure that your topic sentence defines the topic for the reader and states what your opinion about the topic is.

General Writing Topics

Choose as many of these topics as you can to practice your writing. You may work in a small group, with a partner, or on your own.

1. Compare and contrast the situations of Riss and Kline.
2. Classify the different kinds of violence that you have seen in reading these cases.
3. The kinds of violence seen in these stories seems to be escalating in the United States today. Discuss what you, as a citizen, might do to help stem this rise.
4. Define *responsibility* as it applies to your life and your family.

Extra Writing Practice: Quotation Notation

"This we know: the earth does not belong to man, man belongs to the earth. All things are connected like the blood that unites us all. Man did not weave the web of life, he is merely a strand in it. Whatever he does to the web, he does to himself."
Chief Seattle

Write a short essay, answering the following questions:

1. How does this quotation notation relate to the issues of risk and responsibility?
2. What does this quotation tell you about the underlying beliefs of Chief Seattle?

CHAPTER Two

PARENTING, FAMILIES, AND CHILDREN

Chapter Goals
After studying this chapter, you will be able to:
- Identify and define the essential parts of an essay.
- Follow a general structure for developing an essay.
- Use analogies to make points in supporting an essay thesis.
- Write compare and contrast essays.
- Edit and revise your writing.

Introduction

This chapter focuses on the issues surrounding the concept of family. You will look at how our culture shapes our beliefs about families and identify your own ideas on the subject.

Children and the family occupy a central spot in our cultural hearts. Family is an idea that runs through all parts of our culture—politics, movies, advertisements, holidays, weddings, and funerals. The idea of family as a loving, strong, close-knit unit is promoted by many people in many ways. Yet, in striking contrast to this ideal, the United States has one of the highest rates of divorce, child abuse, and infant mortality in the industrialized world. A typical health and human-services caseworker has 50 to 100 families in trouble at any given time. Cases of domestic violence and abuse seem to be more common and are played out in the press, television, and movies every day.

Along with the concept of family comes the idea of parenting. What is a parent? What does it mean to be a good parent? We have moved beyond the idea in our society of parenting as a biological function. As a society, we enjoy cross-racial, cross-cultural, and single-parent adopting; surrogate parenting, and foster parenting. On the darker side, the legal system deals with issues of parental custody in divorce and has even made provisions for children to "divorce" their parents. It is hard to define so-called good parenting until we come to understand what parenting involves in a complex world with too many variables to name.

Families are legal entities as well as social ones. Marriage is not only a sacred contract but also a legal and financial one. In some states, children are still considered property. Children's rights have become a legal issue as well. How much choice should children have about how they are raised? Under what circumstances can, and should, a child be taken away from his or her parents? What is the responsibility of a parent toward his or her children? These are all questions that the growing legal field of children's rights are trying to answer. The questions are difficult and the answers unclear.

In this chapter, you will explore some of the important issues surrounding families and parenting as you continue to develop your writing skills.

Values: Familial, Cultural, and Regional

How many times have you said something or thought something and realized that you sounded or were thinking exactly like your mother or father? How many times have you smelled something that reminded you of home, or seen a movie or heard a song that touched a chord? These incidents may trigger whole ranges of emotions from happy to sad.

The influence of family and the broader influences of culture and regional background play a strong part in shaping our lives. They often form the very basis of our beliefs, which in turn drive our value system. What is horrifying to one person can be run of the mill to another. What makes sense to you may seem ridiculous to someone else. The tricky part about all of this is that family, culture, and region affect the way we think because they provide us with an automatic set of **unconscious assumptions**. We accept these assumptions—from our families, the media, our religious teaching, education system—without ever really looking at them critically. Consequently, much of what we believe and act on goes unquestioned. When certain basic beliefs are questioned, they can become points of argument or controversy.

Think about the traditional idea of family structure in the United States, with a mother and a father in the home and the mother as primary caretaker of the children. In recent years, the rising divorce rate and increased number of working mothers has caused much debate and forced people to examine their assumptions that "mothers are the best caregivers." The assumption that families must have two parents of opposite sexes to foster a "stable situation" is also being challenged. In fact, the country's citizens and politicians have become engaged in a national debate over what has come to be known as "traditional family values."

Exercise 2.1: What Do You Think?

Think about your ideas about family. You may want to make a list or map your ideas. What things about your own family life do you like and why? What things would you change if you could and why? After you have organized your thoughts, write your definition of an ideal family. Take your time here: this definition is not something that can be done in one or two sentences. Develop your ideas carefully and thoroughly so that your audience will have a clear picture of what you see as the ideal family structure. When you are finished, trade papers with a partner, and compare your ideas. How are they different, and how are they the same? How much of your idea of family stems from your own personal experience? How much is cultural?

Exercise 2.2: Values, TV, and Your Thinking

1. Watch whatever shows you like on television for at least one entire evening. As you watch, consider that television mirrors our society in many ways. Television shows reflect what audiences want to see, and most people want to see things that reinforce their own views of the way the world works. After each show, list the name of the show, the characters, and the events. Then, summarize the cultural assumptions that you saw reflected in each show's theme, content, and characters.

   Example:

   Star Trek portrays beings as either good or bad. The captain, as a figure of authority, is good and almost always selfless. The medical folks are brave and ethical. The Klingons are always the worst. Our society assumes that people in authority should be good and that people in medicine should be above reproach. We believe that criminals have no redeeming features.

2. Write responses to the questions below. Then discuss your ideas with a partner or in a group.

   a. What does it mean to be successful in American culture? What do you mean when you use the term successful? Why? Does your view differ from the general view? How?

   b. How is a so-called *good family* portrayed on TV or in advertisements? How do you define a good family? How are your views the same or different from those reflected on television?

   c. What role should women have in raising children? Why? What role should men have? Why?

d. What is your definition of valuable work?
e. What are some characteristics of an American? Do you suppose the characteristics that you are listing are the same ones that non-Americans would list? Why or why not?

Isms, Biases, and Stereotypes

The point of view that one brings to a situation can be complicated and sometimes contradictory. Being able to see other points of view can open up new interpretations of life.

Ism is a suffix that means "doctrine, system, or theory." Sexism is a system of discrimination based on sex; racism is a system of discrimination based on race; ageism is a system of discrimination based on age. We all know about isms, and at some point many of us have experienced life as it has been determined by an ism. Isms can be dangerous and powerful, especially because they are often invisible. In fact, some isms have become so much a part of our culture that we may be operating under those isms without even being aware of them. Isms can be passed on through family, religion, school, media, government, and so on.

What isms have to do with thinking and writing is simple; they provide reasons. Too often, people fall back on an ism as a way to convince someone (or themselves) of their position—whether it be in speaking to another person, acting in life situations, or writing about ideas. If you are not aware of others' or your own isms, you can get "sucked in" and find yourself relying on them to support your point of view. As writers and thinkers, we need to be ready to recognize isms for what they are and be able to counter them.

Biases are like isms in that they are often unconscious, often powerful, and sometimes dangerous. Isms are usually always destructive, while biases can sometimes be good. A bias is simply a kind of favoritism, and that can be positive or negative. Biases exist in cultures, institutions, and organizations, as well as in individuals. It is important to understand biases because they can cloud your thinking and writing. For example, a judge who has a definite bias toward women as caretakers is less likely to award custody to fathers than a judge who is not biased.

Biases can be very obvious and easy to spot, but they are often unacknowledged. Unacknowledged biases occur in situations such as when an organization seems to have only certain kinds of people in it. There may not be anything written down that you can point to to show the bias, but the actions of the organization speak louder than any words they may write or speak.

Stereotypes are classifications of people or ideas based on superficial traits. Stereotypes do not take into consideration individual differences; rather, they are broad, usually inaccurate, generalizations about groups, individuals, events, organizations, or institutions. They can be destructive, and, more often than not, they are offensive. Stereotypes come in such forms as racial slurs, bad jokes about ethnic groups and occupations, and assumptions about lifestyle and place.

Stereotypes can have very real, very deadly consequences. Hate groups, street gangs, injustices, and prejudices are all fueled by belief in and acceptance of stereotypes. Like biases, stereotypes are not always obvious. They can become such a part of a society's, an individual's, or a family's way of thinking that they become almost invisible. It is important to recognize and avoid stereotypes in our own writing and thinking. Some ways to recognize isms, biases, and stereotypes are:

1. Look for connotations and denotations.
2. Look for negative and positive statements that generalize.
3. Look for tone (how the statement is said).
4. Look for actions and outcomes, and evaluate them.

Exercise 2.3: Free Your Mind

We can free ourselves of isms, biases, and stereotypes by recognizing them and discussing them with others. Read each statement below, and ask yourself how you feel about it. What are your beliefs based on? Are you aware of other points of view on the subject? What is your feeling about people who hold those points of view? Discuss the statements in a group, and listen respectfully to all points of view.

1. Working mothers are not as able to give quality care to their children as mothers who stay at home.
2. Two parents are always better than one.
3. Girls are better in reading, and boys are better in math.
4. Children are better off with their biological parents.
5. Institutional day care is not as good as home care.
6. Stay-at-home fathers are not as effective in child rearing as stay-at-home mothers.
7. Living in an urban neighborhood is preferable to living in the suburbs.
8. Families who pray together stay together.

Essays: Not Just for Tests

Many people think of essays as something that they have to write to pass an English test. In fact, essay writing occurs fairly often in everyday life. An **essay** is any short piece of writing on one subject, usually written from a personal point of view. Traditional essays appear in the opinion sections of newspapers and magazines.

Many types of letters have the same components as essays. Most nonpersonal letters are written to persuade someone to do something. For example, when you write a job-application letter, you want to persuade the company to invite you for an interview. There are also many types of essays that are "loosely" persuasive but follow other kinds of forms. These are **compare and contrast essays, cause and effect essays, classification essays, process essays** and others. Each form is suited to a particular purpose.

Elements of a Good Essay

There are certain elements that almost everyone agrees should be included in a well-written essay:

1. **Essays should have a thesis**. A **thesis** is the main point that the writer is making. A thesis is an opinion that is arguable, that is, it makes a point that someone could disagree with. A thesis should be stated clearly as an opinion, not a fact. It should not be announced. For example, the statement, "Women do not make better parents than men" is a thesis. "This paper will attempt to prove that women do not make better parents than men" is not a thesis; it is an announcement. A thesis, because it is, by definition an opinion, should not be phrased like this: "I don't think women make better parents than men." The "I don't think" is redundant: if the writer states the thesis, it is evident that is what the writer thinks.

2. **Essays should take the audience into account**. Readers have certain needs and expectations. Audiences expect, for example, to be told somewhere early on in the essay what the point of reading the essay is (this is the thesis). They expect the essay to make sense, to be logical. They expect the author to connect ideas within the essay by using transitions (connecting words) that show the relationships among ideas. They expect that the author will summarize or conclude at the end of the essay and wrap up all the ideas for the reader. They have these expectations because most writers do these things, so readers expect all writers to do them. When these expectations are not met, readers are in trouble. They become confused as they read, and they struggle to make sense of the writing. As you learn about essays and how to write them, it is important to pay attention to introductions and conclusions, organization of ideas, and transitions between ideas in an essay.

3. **Essays should present evidence to support the thesis.** If you claim that something is good, bad, wonderful, weird, fun, or anything else, you must back up your claim with proof of some sort. This is what essays do: they state an opinion, and they show the reader why this opinion is valid. This means that you will want to have many examples, details, evidence, statistics— whatever it takes to convince the reader of the validity of your thesis. This is called **thesis development.** You also need to learn to fully develop your ideas. We will discuss development in detail in Chapter Three.

Exercise 2.4: The Thesis Statement

Look at the statements below. In the blanks, write "T" if the statement is a thesis, "A" if it is an announcement, and "F" if it is a fact. Then, reword each non-thesis statement to make it into a thesis.

1. _____ Families consist of parents and children.
2. _____ This paper will argue that families are the basis of our society.
3. _____ Parents have a responsibility to their children.
4. _____ I think that children should obey their parents.
5. _____ Parents who abuse their children should have their children taken away from them.

Good Essay Form

There are four essential parts that an essay must have: an introduction, a thesis statement, a body, and a conclusion.

1. The **introduction** does two things: it introduces the reader to the topic, and it leads to the thesis. There are many ways to introduce a topic. You can begin an essay by telling a story that illustrates the thesis you are trying to prove. If your thesis, for example, is that women do not make better parents than men, a story about an excellent father might be a way into the thesis. You could instead begin with a quote that points to your thesis. You might also start by "going in the back door"— by stating the opposing point of view. You might say, "Most people think that men are not as capable of being good parents as women." You could talk about that idea for a while, and then lead to your thesis. You might even find some startling statistic about the difference between fathers and mothers. Any of these introductory strategies will grab your readers' attention, which is just what you want to happen.

2. The **thesis** does two things: it establishes the topic and it says something about that topic. The thesis should be clearly stated, usually in a single sentence called a **thesis statement.** This statement is usually, but not always, the last sentence in the introductory paragraph.

3. The **body** of the essay is where you use examples, logic, data, and other methods to support your thesis. As you work through this book, you will be practicing ways to make your evidence strong and convincing.

If you have more than one piece of evidence for your claim, put each one in a different paragraph. It is usually best to start with your weakest argument and work to your strongest. Save the zingers for the end. For example, you want to make a case for fathers receiving custody of children. Your research has found that 95 percent of all single parents are women and that four out of five women who are single mothers now wished that the fathers had been given custody. The first piece of evidence is not surprising, but the second piece is a zinger.

4. The **conclusion** leads the reader back to the thesis. Do not put any new information here. You may use some of the strategies discussed in the section about introductions. For example, you can end with a story that illustrates the point or you can continue the story you began in the introduction. You may want to end with a particularly apt quote from a good source. You may raise a question or suggest solutions to the problem you have been discussing. The idea is to wrap it up for the reader.

One way to remember and to improve your ability to use these components in your essays is to look for them when you are reading essays. As you read an essay, look for the thesis and underline it. Place an asterisk or some other mark next to statements of the evidence presented. Look carefully at how the writer introduced the topic and concluded the piece. Finally, you may wish to write a sentence that describes how the writer took into account the audience. Reading other people's writing critically and marking it up will often strengthen your own writing skills.

Exercise 2.5: Mark It Up

Read the essay below and mark it up.

Dogs Are Family Members Too

The other day while I was visiting a friend of mine, she told me her dog had died. Feeling very sad, she said it was like losing a member of the family. "But Betty," I insisted, "it's not like losing a member of the family; you did lose a member of your family." Betty wasn't so sure.

I know that many people have many different definitions of what makes up a family. In some cultures families are not just blood relatives or adopted children, but the whole village. In other cultures families are seen as only parents and children. However, I say that when a family has a dog, that dog is a member of the family.

Families are social units whose members care about each other. Family members take care of each other. Family members learn from each other. They have good times and bad times, but they usually tough it out. In our culture the immediate family often lives together. Dogs do all these things. Dogs certainly care about the family, protect the family, enjoy the family, and bring pleasure to the family. Dogs live with the family.

Some people would say "Dogs don't teach us anything" or "Dogs don't understand what's going on so they can't be full members of the family" or "Only people can be members of families." I disagree. Dogs remind us to have fun, to not take life so seriously. This is an important thing to learn. And while it's true that dogs don't understand what is going on in the family, children often do not either. Children are certainly family members. Finally, why limit our vision of family to creatures just like ourselves? Everyone in a family contributes in a unique way. While dogs are different they still do many of the things that other members do—they just do it with a twist.

Betty was very sad that her family lost their dog. I was sad too that they had lost a member who protected them, made them laugh, challenged them, loved them and was loved by them. In other words, they lost a family member because dogs are family members too.

Compare and Contrast Essays

In **compare and contrast essays**, the evidence and explanation of the thesis are developed by examining the similarities and differences between at least two things. To **compare** means to look at similarities. To **contrast** means to look at differences.

For example, you could compare and contrast your upbringing with that of your parents to clarify and strengthen your thesis that children in the past were raised differently from children nowadays. You could compare families in one country with families in another. You could look within this country and compare and contrast families from different ethnic groups. The possibilities are endless.

When you write a thesis for a compare and contrast essay, it should make a specific point about the comparison you are making. For instance, a statement that says, "There are many similarities and differences between the way I was raised and the way my mother was raised" does not make any point. In fact, who cares? You could say there are similarities and differences between *any* two things—even identical twins. Rather, you compare and contrast things so that the reader learns something important about them. A better thesis would be, "Although my mother tried to raise me the way she was raised, she was unsuccessful because her generation had a stricter upbringing than did mine."

There are basically two ways to structure a compare and contrast essay. Let's say you are comparing A with B. You can (1) state everything about A and then compare and contrast everything about B or (2) do a point-by-point discussion. In the first case, you would have a long section on A, discussing points 1,2,3,4, and 5; then you would have a long section on B, also discussing points 1,2,3,4, and 5. This would be followed by a conclusion that would sum up and restate your thesis. Using the second way, you would have a paragraph on point 1, comparing and contrasting A with B; a paragraph on point 2, comparing and contrasting A with B; a paragraph on point 3, comparing and contrasting A with B; and so on. See the example outlines on the next page:

COMPARE/CONTRAST BY THINGS TO BE COMPARED

1. Introduction
   Thesis: *Although my mother tried to raise me the way she was raised, she was unsuccessful because she had a stricter upbringing than I.*
2. My mother's upbringing
   a. respect for elders
   b. total obedience
   c. work: helped support the family
   d. a code of ethics within the family
3. My upbringing
   a. respect for elders: not so much
   b. obedience: at times—lots of rebellion
   c. work: for myself/my own money
   d. a code of ethics: more loyalty to my friends than to my family
4. Conclusion

COMPARE/CONTRAST BY POINTS OF COMPARISON

1. Introduction
2. Respect for elders
   a. my mother: total respect
   b. me: not much left
3. Obedience
   a. my mother: total obedience or else
   b. me: breaking rules and learning consequences
4. Work
   a. my mother: gave earnings to family to help out
   b. me: what I earn is mine to keep and play with
5. Code of ethics
   a. my mother: family is everything—even having bad thoughts about family is betrayal
   b. me: friends are more important, and family can be criticized
6. Conclusion

Either structure works well for compare and contrast essays, but there are different ways to use them. For a short paper, the first form is fine. You can assume as a writer that your readers will remember everything you have said about your mother when they get to the section about you. But if the paper is a long one, the reader may become lost and not remember everything. In that case, you might want to choose the second form. Think of it this way: the structure of your essay should help the readers not confuse them. Therefore, use the structure that makes the most sense to you.

Essay Topic: Child Support

Child support is another of the many sticky issues surrounding parents and parenting in our society. The question of who pays, how much, when and for how long is a constant battle that is played out in the courts everyday. It is also a question that stirs up many emotions including anger, outrage, and disgust. Recently, the issue of child support has become politicized. Titles such as "Dead Beat Dads" (*Newsweek* 1992) and "Making Delinquent Dad Pay His Child Support" (*Ms.* 1992) appeared on the covers of major news magazines. State and federal legislators are proposing new laws in this area.

Is that all there is? Is child support and the attached issue of parenting a cut-and-dried legal problem? How are those issues reflected in the value system of our culture as well as in our personal beliefs? Below are two cases. Read them and be the judge and jury. After each case, there are some questions to help you analyze the case. Each case will offer you a chance to respond to questions and write an essay response. After reading, thinking, and writing about both cases, you will write a compare and contrast essay about the different perspectives on child care that these cases highlight.

CASE STUDY 1:

Edith Maude Hendry v. Joe B. Hendry, Jr.

Joe and Edith Hendry were divorced in 1968. At that time, they reached a child support settlement in which Mr. Hendry agreed to pay Mrs. Hendry $500 per month. Their daughter, 4 at the time of the divorce, was 11 years old when Mrs. Hendry filed a "modification petition" and asked for an increase in her child support payments. Mr. Hendry's financial situation had improved in the intervening years, and the cost of living had escalated. Mrs. Hendry felt that her daughter deserved more money as her "needs had increased with her age."

Mrs. Hendry, although a naturalized U.S. citizen, had lived in Amsterdam and Beirut in the intervening years since her divorce. She felt it was important for her daughter to be able to visit her grandparents in Europe once a year. In addition, the child's new expenses included tennis lessons for $100 a month, summer camp for $500-$600 per month, and the tuition at Palm Beach Day School at $2,050 per year. The child, who spoke four languages at the time, could no longer be accommodated in the public school system where she had been for the last two years. The cost of all these necessities was not anticipated when the child was 4. The $500 a month originally awarded no longer covered the child's needs.

Mr. Hendry argued that his net worth had diminished rather than increased. Therefore, increased payments of child support could not be based upon an increase in his wealth: his net worth fell from $3.1 million in 1967 to $2.8 million by mid-1975. Another issue that needed to be addressed was the question of whether these additional expenses were in the "best interest" of the child or were they frivolous? The court had to decide whether Mr. Hendry should have to pay increased child support payments to his ex-wife.

This case was ultimately tried at two levels with two different decisions. The first decision was in favor of Mr. Hendry, and the second decision was in favor of Mrs. Hendry.

Exercise 2.6: Essay Practice

1. To get a solid understanding of your perspective on the Hendry case, write a short response to each of the questions below. You may also want to discuss your responses with a partner.

   a. What are the kinds of things that parents are responsible for providing to their children? Are they just responsible for providing the basic necessities of life, or must they open the doors of opportunity as widely as possible for their children? What does it mean in everyday life to create opportunity as widely as possible?

   b. How do you define basic necessities? What assumptions do you make when you define those necessities? (Be careful: your biases may be showing.)

   c. How does your own background figure into your responses? (Any stereotypes or isms here?)

2. If you were the judge in this case, what would you have decided and why? What do you think the key issue in your decision would be? Write out your decision in a short essay. Don't forget to use the prewriting and writing strategies you learned in Chapter One.

CASE STUDY 2:

Tammy Lynne Hernandez v. Miguel Carlos Hernandez

Miguel, who taught in an alternative school for troubled high school kids in the city of Houston, and his wife Tammy Lynne, a waitress, were divorced in 1980. Their one daughter Regina, an infant at the time of the breakup, had been receiving child support of $150 a month for five years. The child had displayed unusual musical talent, but Tammy Lynne could not afford violin lessons, which cost $60 a month. She had been planning to return to the local community college to earn a two-year's degree in nursing so she could find a better job and provide Regina with more opportunities.

At the time of the case, Tammy Lynne earned $15,000 per year as a waitress in an elegant restaurant. She and her daughter lived with her mother, who took care of Regina when Tammy Lynne was at work. Tammy Lynne made regular contributions to her mother's household, bought groceries, and helped to pay the taxes. In order for Tammy to attend the nursing program at the local community college she had to cut her waitressing hours by half. She was still able to work during the holidays and in the summer, but she expected her income to drop to around $7,000 per year. If she attended school on a part-time basis, it would take at least three years to finish the nursing program.

Tammy Lynne filed a petition of modification for an increase in child support of $100 a month to pay for Regina's music lessons and offset Tammy Lynne's school expenses which would run approximately $250 a month. She also wanted Miguel to buy Regina a violin at a one-time cost of $1,000.

Miguel had remarried within the last year, and his present wife was pregnant. They owned their own home, and their mortgage payments, including taxes, were $600 per month. His wife had recently finished her teaching degree and had $10,000 worth of school loans to pay off. She was doing substitute teaching, which paid $30 per day, but the work was erratic. Miguel earned $27,000 a year and was also working on the 30 credit hours he needed for permanent certification in the state of Texas. He contended that his financial situation had not improved; in fact, it had decreased given his new responsibilities and his need for additional schooling. He had already taken on summer employment as a camp counselor for physically challenged children in an attempt to meet his child-support payments during the summer and earn extra income.

Exercise 2.7: Compare and Contrast Essay

1. Write and/or discuss responses to the questions below.

    a. How much responsibility does a biological parent have to support his or her child if the parent does not help raise the child?

    b. Are the kinds of things the Hernandezes want to provide for their child the same as those the Hendrys want? Are they basic necessities or frills?

    c. Should Tammy Lynne receive more money from her ex-husband so that she can improve her own status and afford violin lessons for Regina? Is access to opportunity a basic necessity? How does society define opportunity and decide who gets it?

    d. Is Miguel's education equally as important as Tammy's?

e. In looking at these questions, did you keep in mind your own background and any biases, isms, or stereotypes that might affect your point of view? Consider the following:

1) What assumptions do you make about the characters in each of these stories? Does money figure into your reactions to these characters? How about geography? Does it matter to you that one couple is poor and a minority and the other is rich?

2) Are there experiences you have had that cause you to respond in a particular way (for example, do you feel you were deprived of certain opportunities? Have you had to pay what you consider to be outrageous child support?)

2. If you were the judge in this case, what would you decide and why? What do you think the key issue in your decision would be? Use freewriting to put your ideas on paper.

3. Now that you have read, thought about, and possibly discussed the two child-support cases, you should have a good idea about how you feel about the reasons for child support and the financial responsibilities parents have for their children. Write a compare and contrast essay on the Hernandez and Hendry cases to defend a thesis statement. If you need help thinking of a thesis, you can use one of the theses below. Take your time. Map out your ideas, and use fact patterns. Then review the two possible forms you can use to structure your essay. Choose the one you feel is most suitable, and write. You may wish to share your draft with a partner to get feedback.

POSSIBLE THESES FOR COMPARE/CONTRAST ESSAYS:

(Keep in mind that you could also argue the opposite of any of these thesis statements.)

a. Both parents, regardless of income, are responsible for providing for their children all opportunities for growth and advancement that they can provide. This thesis needs to address questions such as:

- How does income affect what we see as basic necessities?
- What are opportunities for growth and advancement?
- How do parents offer their children opportunities?
- Do parents with larger incomes owe more to their children than parents with smaller incomes?

b. The responsibility of a parent providing child support is to help the child maintain the lifestyle that she or he had at the time of separation. (Compare Hendry's responsibility with Hernandez's.)

c. Whenever a parent providing child support has a change in income, the child-support payments should change in the same way.

Metaphors, Similes, Analogies

When writing comparisons, you want to use language that is strong, clear, and concise. Your reader will lose interest if you use too many words or vague, general terms to make your point. A common tool in writing comparative essays is the use of metaphors, similes, and analogies. Every great writer, politician, playwright, and public speaker uses them to bring their ideas to life. They help your audience grasp your meaning in interesting and powerful ways.

A **metaphor** is a word or phrase meaning one thing that is used in place of another to suggest a likeness between them. For example, "All the world's a stage" is a metaphor that compares life to the drama of a theatrical play. Metaphors often compare an abstract idea to a concrete object or to something that is common in the everyday. Why? The abstraction is usually the difficult thing to define and understand, while most people know about the concrete object.

A **simile** is a comparison when the words like or as are used. A metaphor says "This is that," but a simile says "This is like that:" for example, "My love is like a rose."

Similes and metaphors are two kinds of analogies. An **analogy** compares the similarities of one thing to another. Analogies are always open to interpretation, and exaggeration in analogies is common. A good analogy is one that creates a clear picture in the reader's mind. It should use ideas that are familiar to most people, whether or not they agree with the point being made.

Look at the following list of analogies. Which ones do you think are vivid and can be universally understood? Discuss them in a group to see what others think.

1. The nineties are like the sixties all over again.
2. Mount St. Helens erupted like a champagne bottle.
3. The obliteration of the rain forest removes the lungs of the planet.
4. Life is like a box of chocolates.
5. He came on like a week in the Bahamas.
6. The road to hell is paved with good intentions.
7. She is like the wind beneath my wings.
8. To say that "It is better to have loved and lost than never to have loved at all" is like saying "It is better to have driven your car off a cliff than never to have driven at all.

PARENTING, FAMILIES, AND CHILDREN

Exercise 2.8: Writing Analogies

Write at least three analogies about something that you would like other people to understand. It could be an experience you had or something about your life. If you prefer, pick a topic from the list below. When writing analogies be creative, but be accurate as well. Sloppy analogies or metaphors don't work so well. Avoid overused expressions such as "It's as hard as a rock" or "It's like springtime in Paris."

1. Babies are…
2. Keeping kids out of trouble is like…
3. Being an only child is like…
4. Thanksgiving at my house is…
5. Understanding kids today is like…
6. My family is like…

After you have written your analogies, discuss them with a partner.

Exercise 2.9: Extra Essay Practice

1. Look back to Chapter One at the *Farwell v. Keaton* case (page 25). In that case, Farwell's father sued his son's friend for not assisting his son in a reasonable and responsible way. In *Hendry v. Hendry*, Mrs. Hendry argued that her former husband had certain responsibilities to his daughter. How is the issue of responsibility between friends and between family members similar? How is it different?

Write a compare and contrast essay that explores these issues, using the two cases. Make sure your draft has an introduction, a conclusion, and follows compare and contrast form. Use analogies where you can to make your points.

THESIS SUGGESTIONS:
1. Parents have long-term responsibility for children, but people generally have responsibility only for friends and others in emergency situations.
2. Individuals have responsibilities only to assist others in emergencies.
3. When your essay is finished, find a partner and exchange essays. Locate the analogies in your partner's essay, and analyze them to see if they work. Do the analogies add to the piece, or do they seem to be out of place? If that is the case, give your partner suggestions on how to use the analogy in a better way or to change it altogether.

CHAPTER REVIEW
Putting It All Together

Think back over what you have done in Chapters One and Two. This is an opportunity to pull everything together and practice what you have learned.

Below is a list of possible writing topics. Choose one of these topics, and write a compare and contrast essay. As you do so, keep in mind the following steps:

1. Organize your ideas and materials, using mapping and other prewriting strategies.
2. Choose a structure that works best for you.
3. Make sure that you have included all the essential components of an essay.
4. Before considering your draft as final, go through the revision process below.

Revision Checklist

This process works best when you trade papers with another person. Read over the other person's paper, and answer the following questions.

1. Underline the thesis. Does it announce the topic? Does it make a point about the topic?
2. Does the introduction grab the reader's interest? If not, try to suggest ways the writer might rewrite the introduction following the advice on page 36.
3. List the writer's supporting evidence for the thesis. Is it valid? Can you add any more? Suggest additional ideas to the writer, if you can.
4. Does the writer use examples and explain them carefully?
5. Does the conclusion sum up the point of the essay?
6. Has the writer interjected his or her personal opinions or isms, biases, or stereotypes? Call attention to any problems here if necessary.

General Writing Topics

Choose one of the essay topics (theses) below, and write a polished compare and contrast essay. Writing a polished essay means taking your time planning what you are going to write. Develop a thesis statement, and decide what form you are going to use to compare and contrast. Write a draft, share the draft with a partner, and then rewrite the draft. Go through this process until you are satisfied that your essay is polished. Remember, good writers always rewrite. Feel free to amend any of these theses or come up with your own.

1. America is a better place to raise a family than it was 50 years ago.
2. America is a worse place to live than it was 50 years ago.
3. My neighborhood is a better/worse place to live than it used to be.
4. It is better for children to move out of the house after the age of 20 than it is for them to stay at home.
5. Families are stronger when the grandparents live with or near their children.
6. Single parenting is much harder than parenting with a partner.

Extra Writing Practice: Quotation Notation

"In every dispute between parent and child, both cannot be right, but they may be, and usually are, both wrong. It is this situation which gives family life its peculiar hysterical charm."
Isaac Rosenfeld

Write a compare and contrast essay that either supports or disputes this thesis.

CHAPTER Three

PRIVACY, CONFIDENTIALITY, AND THE RIGHT TO KNOW

Chapter Goals

After studying this chapter, you will be able to:

- Understand how to use cause and effect to organize information.
- Use a cause/effect structure to develop written essays.
- Understand the importance of using details when writing.
- Use details to write cause-and-effect essays.

Introduction

This chapter focuses on the issues of privacy, confidentiality, and the right to know. You will once again look at your own beliefs and values and see how they shape your understanding of these ideas.

Exactly what do we mean by *privacy, confidentiality*, and the *right to know*? What parts of our lives can we reasonably assume to be private—no one's business other than our own? If you have children of your own, how do you encourage them to be honest with you, even when it comes to tough topics such as drugs and sex? In turn, as a parent, to what degree should you and can you maintain the confidentiality of your children and their friends? If something is told to you in confidence, but you know that the information could harm someone, should you keep it a secret or should you tell some authority such as a teacher, minister, or police officer?

Privacy, confidentiality, and the right to know all have legal significance. For example, there are laws that prevent landlords from entering a tenant's apartment without notice. There are laws that govern the confidential relationship between doctor and patient, priest and confessor, and lawyer and client. There are laws that govern the public's "right to know." For instance, the information about the ingredients in packaged foods and the warning labels on cigarettes, alcohol, and over-the-counter medicines are the result of laws governing the right to know.

People have come to believe that the Constitution guarantees many of these rights when, in fact, it does not. For instance, the Constitution of the United States does not anywhere specifically state that individuals have a right to privacy. The Fourth Amendment guarantees individuals the right to be "secure, in their persons, houses, papers and effects, against unreasonable searches and seizures." The Fourteenth Amendment says that the state cannot deprive anyone of life, liberty, or property without due process of law. Privacy, then, is "guaranteed" by the overlap of the Fourth and Fourteenth Amendments. The First Amendment guarantees freedom of speech. Thus, the "right to know" is an outcome of the media's and citizens' right to disseminate information freely

This chapter will examine these ideas and how they directly affect your life and the lives of people just like you across the country.

Values: Are You How You Behave?

Take a minute or two to think about your behavior as it reflects your value system. For instance, how do you act "when the going gets tough"? When you get into a difficult situation or have to make a decision about something, does your behavior always reflect what you believe to be "right" and "wrong"? How often does your behavior seem to be in conflict with what you believe to be your core value system?

The issues that arise around values and how they relate to behavior are complicated. For example, in most societies being loyal is considered "good," while being a traitor is "bad." A person is expected to be loyal to country, family, and friends. Loyalties are not supposed to be betrayed, and often the price of betrayal is high. What happens, then, when an individual is expected to be loyal to conflicting groups?

Consider the following situation. In most schools, cheating on a test is grounds for suspension. However, students who report students, or "snitch," can find themselves with a black eye and no friends as a reward for their "good behavior." There are two conflicting value systems at work here. The first value system, "cheating on a test is wrong," belongs to the institution; the second, "don't tell on your friends," belongs to the students within the institution. The second value of "not informing" (being loyal to one's friends) can and usually does override the first (cheating is bad and one should be loyal to the institution). The acceptable behavior, in this case, is that students have to be caught red-handed by someone in authority and not turned in by a friend.

This same scenario often happens with issues of confidentiality and privacy. Almost everyone, at some time in his or her life, will be told a secret that creates a conflict between values and behavior. This can happen on a personal as well as a professional level. What the person does with that secret is always a tough decision. It becomes tricky when an individual's health or safety is at stake. The famous example that often comes to mind is the priest who learns of a murder during confession and is sworn to confidentiality under the laws of the church.

As you can see by these simple examples, the issues of privacy, confidentiality, and the right to know can become extremely complicated. You have seen here and elsewhere in this book how our values and beliefs are reflected in our behavior and the way we react to situations.

Exercise 3.1: Valuing Privacy

1. Following is a list of statements that focus on privacy issues and the values that may conflict with them. Mark them T for true or F for false. Base your responses on what you value, not what you think the world, your friends, or your teachers value. (This is not a test; keep your responses private, if you like.)

    _____ Individuals should be able to do whatever they want in the privacy of their homes.

    _____ Never betray a friend.

    _____ Gossip is usually wrong and not worth listening to.

    _____ Government has the obligation to inform the public about what it does with the taxpayers' money.

    _____ You should not have to tell the new person in your life about past relationships.

    _____ What you do with your friends is your business.

    _____ Always knock before entering.

    _____ Honesty is the best policy, even when it may hurt someone.

    _____ A child's room is his or her special place and should be left alone.

    _____ A doctor should always tell the patient everything, even when the news is terrible.

2. Think about your responses to the statements and what they tell you about yourself. Look at your answers and see if you can find some connections. For example, do you find yourself valuing confidentiality but only within certain limits?

    Write a two-or three-paragraph piece on how your responses reflect your feelings about privacy, confidentiality, and the right to know. (This is a good place to practice some of the definition-and-summary work you did in Chapter One.)

Cause and Effect

Throughout this book, you have been learning how to organize, think, and write about information in different ways. In Chapter Two, you used the method of comparing and contrasting information and ideas. Another way to organize and write about information and ideas is to look for cause and effect.

If you were to tip over your chair right this minute and make a loud noise, you would be demonstrating a cause-and-effect relationship. **Cause** is anything that makes something else happen; the thing that happens is the **effect**. In the above example, tipping your chair over is the cause, and the loud noise is the effect. Causes and effects can be very straightforward, as in the chair and the noise. They can also be very elusive and complicated, almost like a puzzle.

Causal Relationships

In a nutshell, **causal thinking**, or looking for **causal relationships**, boils down to answering the questions "how?" or "why?" Once you figure out how or why something happens, you gain a better understanding of the situation and you can make better decisions about it.

On the surface, causal relationships seem uncomplicated. However, not everyone agrees on what causes what. Consider that lawsuits and academic debates are built around arguing about cause and effect.

The following exercise will help you see that figuring out causal relationships is not always easy.

Exercise 3.2: Finding Causal Relationships

For each of the circumstances listed, state a cause and an effect. You may give more than one answer. You may do this exercise alone or with a partner.

Example

Police must have a search warrant or "reasonable cause" before they can look for evidence of a crime.

CAUSE:

People have a right to privacy and to freedom from harassment by police. There must be reason to suspect that a crime or evidence of a crime will be found.

EFFECT:

Criminals have time to destroy evidence; sometimes, evidence cannot be used in court.

1. A deceased person's safe-deposit box may not be opened without permission from the court.
   CAUSE: _____
   _____
   EFFECT: _____
   _____

2. Manufacturers must print the surgeon general's warning about health risks on cigarette packages and alcohol labels.
   CAUSE: _____
   _____
   EFFECT: _____
   _____

3. Doctors are not allowed to tell family members that a patient has a serious contagious disease without the permission of the patient.
   CAUSE: _____
   _____
   EFFECT: _____
   _____

4. A member of a jury may not discuss the case with anyone until after deliberations and the end of the trial.
   CAUSE: _____
   _____
   EFFECT: _____
   _____

5. Journalists do not have to reveal the names of sources who give them information pertaining to a crime.
   CAUSE: _____
   _____
   EFFECT: _____
   _____

6. Ingredients must be listed on labels of cans and packages of food.
   CAUSE: _____
   _____
   EFFECT: _____
   _____

7. People must be warned of danger with signs that say "proceed at your own risk" or "use at your own risk."
   CAUSE: _____
   _____
   EFFECT: _____
   _____

8. The police may legally record telephone conversations without the knowledge of individuals, under certain circumstances.

   CAUSE: _____

   EFFECT: _____

9. It is a federal offense to open or tamper with other people's mail.

   CAUSE: _____

   EFFECT: _____

10. Unsolicited statements from a dying person are considered admissible evidence in a court proceeding.

    CAUSE: _____

    EFFECT: _____

Causal Connections

As you probably just discovered, causal relationships can be pretty complicated. In fact, the equation A causes B is rare. Within most situations, there are several causal relationships that overlap and become tangled.

Sometimes, causal relationships exist **sequentially**; that is, A causes B which causes C which causes D and so forth. For example, an earthquake causes your chair to shake, which causes it to tip over, which causes you to fall out of it creating a loud noise.

Other times, causal relationships exist **simultaneously**; that is A causes B, and C causes D, but the combination results in E. For example, you need to change the lightbulb (A), so you are standing on a chair (B). The earth shifts (C), which causes an earthquake (D). The fact that you are standing on a chair during an earthquake causes the chair to tip and make a loud noise (E). Learning how to organize causal relationships by finding sequential and simultaneous connections will help your writing and thinking.

The following case study deals specifically with issues of privacy. It will give you practice in sorting out causal connections.

CASE STUDY 1:
Griswold v. The United States

On November 1, 1961, the state of Connecticut's Planned Parenthood League opened a clinic at 82 Trumbull Street, in New Haven. The executive director of the league was Estelle Trebert Griswold, age 61. The medical director of the clinic was Charles Lee Buxton, age 57. Buxton was also the chairman of the Obstetrics Department at Yale University Medical School.

The planned opening of the New Haven clinic was in direct defiance of an 82-year-old Connecticut law. The law made the use of birth-control devices illegal. This, in turn, made providing information about birth control and using birth-control devices a criminal offense. Doctors and medical personnel could be prosecuted if caught giving out birth-control information. Individuals could be prosecuted if caught using birth-control products or devices.

Nine days after the clinic opened, the police arrested Buxton and Griswold and closed the clinic. They were charged and convicted in the circuit court. They were each sentenced to pay a $100 fine. This did not stop Griswold and Buxton. They immediately reopened the clinic. The police arrested them again. This time, they appealed to the state supreme court. The original judgment was upheld. Finally, the Griswold and Buxton case was argued in front of the United States Supreme Court on March 29, 1965. It became one of the landmark decisions concerning an individual's constitutional right of privacy.

"This is basically a civil rights issue and [an issue of] rights that are denied to women," Griswold declared. "It's the same old story, women of influence and means get therapeutic treatment denied to the poor.... Women of influence and means can get the treatment because they know someone or can go out of state."

Griswold's sentiments were echoed by Buxton: "Clinical patients deserve the same access to this information [about birth control] as private patients," said Buxton. "The physical and mental health of married women in Connecticut will best be served by the administration of contraceptive advice to those who need it."

The Griswold/Buxton case attacked the Connecticut law as an invasion of an individual's right of privacy. The argument focused on the question of who should make decisions about birth control, women (or couples) or the state of Connecticut. The Griswold case was founded on the argument that the government had no "place" in the bedroom, one of the most private areas of an individual's life.

Griswold won the case, and the decision stands as a landmark in beginning the legal definition of privacy and the rights of women regarding the reproductive process.

Exercise 3.3: Finding Causal Connections

There are many causal connections in this case. See how many you can find by answering the questions below. You may do this exercise alone or with a partner. When you are finished, compare your answers to the answers at the end of the book.

1. What do you think are the causes that "drove" Buxton and Griswold to open the clinic and purposely get arrested? List at least three.
2. Are any of the causes you listed related to moral or ethical issues? What values are reflected by these issues?
3. Of the causes that you have listed, which one do you think is the most important and why?
4. What is the overall effect of the outcome of the Griswold case?

Cause-and-Effect Essays

Now that you have a basic understanding of cause-and-effect relationships, it is time to put them to work in your writing. The **cause-and-effect essay**, just like the compare and contrast essay, is a way of persuading a reader that your point of view is a valid one. Think of how lawyers use causal reasoning all the time to convince juries to convict or acquit accused defendants.

Cause-and-effect essays are basically structured very simply, even when the causal relationships are complex. First, you need to decide whether you are going to talk about causes or about effects. Unless you are writing a very long piece, it is better to stick to only one side of the causal relationship.

Whether you decide to talk about causes or effects, the essay uses the same general structure.

Causes or Effects

INTRODUCTION: *The introduction gives some background about what you are writing. It helps to orient the reader, and it should set the tone of the essay.*

THESIS: *The thesis states your main idea: X was **caused** by the following things **or** X has the following **effects**.*

EVIDENCE PARAGRAPH: *Cause 1 or Effect 1*

EVIDENCE PARAGRAPH: *Cause 2 or Effect 2*

EVIDENCE PARAGRAPH: *Cause 3 or Effect 3*

CONCLUSION: *This part of the essay needs to bring the reader right back around to where you started and should be written with a good deal of conviction. There is no time for "wishy-washy" language here. Do not add any new material.*

Below you will find a model essay written about the Griswold case. It is marked up so that you can see how the writer followed the cause-and-effect essay structure. Notice how she used the details in the case and expanded on them and explained them so that her audience would understand her point better. Notice that she even quoted from the story to prove her point.

Example:

One of the most impressive things about Estelle Griswold is her courage and her belief in her own convictions. <u>Griswold was quite willing to go to jail, be fined, and become a public figure to force the courts to examine the issue of privacy</u>. She valued equal access to medical treatment for all women. She felt that the Connecticut law should be repealed and she was willing to fight for it. — Thesis

<u>Griswold believed that all women deserved equal access to birth control</u>. She knew that women who could afford high-priced, private doctors could get whatever they needed. But she also knew that poor women had to rely on public clinics and that the Connecticut laws forbade the sale of and education about birth control. In fact, she said, "It's the same old story, women of influence and means can get therapeutic treatment denied to the poor. . . . Women of influence and means could get the treatment because they knew someone or could go out of state." — first cause / detail / quote from case study

<u>Griswold also believed that women had a right to privacy</u>. She thought that the Connecticut law forbidding birth control in public clinics was an invasion of a woman's right to privacy. She also believed that the government "had no place in the bedroom." This too made her fight for her beliefs. — second cause / quote from case study

Most importantly, <u>Griswold understood that sometimes the only way to get a law changed is to break it</u>. So even though she knew she would be breaking the law by providing birth-control services in the clinic, she was willing to risk fines and a jail sentence. She knew that sometimes the kind of publicity that such "civil disobedience" generates would be the best way to call attention to a problem and get other people to support her. — third cause

So, because Griswold believed strongly in a poor woman having the same access to medical care as a rich woman, because she believed in a woman's right to privacy, and because she believed in civil disobedience, she challenged the Connecticut law. In the long run, she won.

Exercise 3.4: Essay Practice

Use the following questions to guide your thinking about the Griswold case. Choose one topic that interests you, and write a cause-and-effect essay. Feel free to go back and look at the model.

1. What do you find most surprising about the Griswold case?
2. Why do you think Estelle Griswold, a middle-aged lady from Connecticut, bothered to get herself arrested and her picture all over the front page of the papers?
3. What motivates people to put themselves in jeopardy to prove a point?
4. What kind of person is Estelle Griswold?
5. Was Griswold correct in breaking the law? Why or why not?
6. Why do you think the United States Supreme Court agreed to hear the case? (Note: The Supreme Court chooses which cases to "hear." There are many more cases that come to the Court than the justices can handle. Some cases are heard and then sent back to the state court for a retrial. Therefore, cases that are actually decided by the Supreme Court are usually very important. What would make this one such a case?)

Exercise 3.5: The Importance of Feedback

There are very few writers in the world who do not rely on feedback from other people about their work. The feedback you get from your classmates, teachers, and friends helps you polish your work and make it better. Find a classmate or friend who is willing to help you. Follow the steps below.

1. Read your work aloud to your partner. Reading aloud lets you hear how your work sounds. It also helps you find mistakes that you may not have noticed.
2. Ask these questions. (Take notes to use in the revision process.)
   What did you like best about the piece?
   What do you want or need to know more about?
   What makes the least sense? Why?
   What would you change if anything?
3. Have your partner read your work and mark it up. In this case, look to see if you have followed the cause/effect essay structure.
4. Have your partner reread your work to help you with spelling and grammar mistakes.
5. Look over your notes and revise your work, taking into account the feedback from your partner.

As you continue writing, keep the revision process in mind. Use it as often as you can to improve your writing. Remember, though, that not everything you write will have a final draft. Sometimes, you may throw things away or keep them for a later time.

Media and the Right to Privacy

The next case deals with a tough issue: the media and an individual's right to privacy. The *legally protected right of privacy* is defined as follows:

the right of an individual to be let alone, or to live a life of seclusion, or to be free from unwarranted publicity, or to live without unwarranted interference by the public about matters with which the public is not necessarily concerned, or to be protected from any wrongful intrusion into an individual's private life which would outrage or cause mental suffering, shame, or humiliation to a person of ordinary sensibilities. (Black, Henry Campbell, Black's Law Dictionary. St. Paul, MN: West Publishing Company, 1990)

When people take on a public role and allow themselves to be photographed and interviewed by the media, and seek public attention by other means, courts have ruled that they are no longer protected by privacy rights laws.

CASE STUDY 2:
Sidis v. F-R Publishing Corporation

William James Sidis was only 11 years old when he gave his very first lecture to a group of professors at Harvard University. He was the child prodigy of Boris Sidis, a famous psychologist, who did research in hypnosis and psychosuggestion. The topic of the boy's talk was "Four-Dimensional Bodies," a subject of great mathematical complexity. There was little doubt in the minds of the audience that the young Sidis would grow up to be a great mathematician.

When William Sidis was born, his father decided to do a series of experiments with his young son. Beginning when his son was 2, Professor Sidis used hypnosis and psychosuggestion to "create" a child wonder. By the time the boy was 5, he had written a paper on anatomy. By the time he was 11, he was a Harvard student. William Sidis's childhood was not composed of sandbox buddies, toys, and tree houses. He had almost no friends and spent most of his time with books, by himself, or with his father. His one recreation was riding streetcars with his parents.

After his lightning start at Harvard, there were stories about his accomplishments on the front pages of the nation's newspapers. He was constantly in demand, and stories about him were read by eager readers. However, the pressure of being a child whiz began to show. He eventually had a nervous breakdown and went to a mental hospital to recover. When he finally returned to Harvard, he became a shy student and refused to lecture again. By the time he was 16, he entered Harvard Law School and was a brilliant but reclusive student. Three years later, at the age of 19, he left Harvard to teach mathematics at a school in Texas. Sidis then turned his life to politics and streetcars. The once child wonder of Harvard became an eccentric and strange young man. He turned his political attentions to organizing demonstrations to support the Communist Party. In his spare time, he collected streetcar transfers. As the years went by, he would "disappear" to lead the "perfect life" of seclusion, only to reappear involved in some outlandish event or demonstration.

He remained out of the public eye until an article appeared in the August 14, 1937, issue of *The New Yorker* magazine. The article detailed much of Sidis's private life and portrayed him as an eccentric living in a shabby South Boston walkup. The article ended with an account of the squalor of Sidis's room, his odd laugh and mannerisms, and his obsession with streetcars and the Okamakammessett Indians. Although the article was a "good read," it was merciless in its dissection of the private life of a once public figure who had consistently sought privacy.

Sidis sued on the grounds that his right to privacy had been violated. He lost. The courts ruled that everyone has a right to privacy about intimate details of his/her life. But public figures surrender that right by being public figures. "His [Sidis] uncommon achievements and personality would have made the attention permissible…. The article in *The New Yorker* sketched the life of an unusual personality, and it possessed considerable popular news interest." The courts also found that *The New Yorker* was not guilty of actual malice in the publication of the Sidis story, an element that must be present to prove libel.

Epilogue: William Sidis died in total poverty at the age of 46. He was found in a coma in a Brookline boarding house and taken to the hospital. He never regained consciousness. His father died in 1924 and can still be found in *Who Was Who in America.* William, despite his early achievements, leaves almost no footprints.

Exercise 3.6: Group Reflection and Discussion

Think about the following questions, and discuss them in a group. You may want to write down your thoughts.

1. If you were Sidis's attorney, how would you argue his case?
2. Why do you think Sidis's life turned out the way it did?
3. Do you believe that public figures give up their right to a private life and, in fact, was Sidis a public figure? Why or why not?
4. What do you think is the proper role of the media in bringing information to the public?
5. What does the Sidis case have in common with television talk shows such as *The Oprah Winfrey Show* and *The Ricki Lake Show* or tabloid news programs such as *Hard Copy* and *A Current Affair*?

Cause and Effect: So What?

You have spent a fair amount of time looking for causal connections. The next step, as you become a more effective writer and reader, is to analyze critically or evaluate causal relationships. You need to ask questions such as, "Did A really cause B, or is that just what someone else thinks or wants me to think?"

In the Sidis case, the causes and the effects are not nearly as clear as they are in the Griswold case. When working with cause-and-effect relationships, you need the ability not only to recognize them, but also to be able to figure out which ones are real and which ones are not. You can practice this with the Sidis case by doing the following exercise.

Exercise 3.7: Cause/Effect Evaluation

In the spaces to the left, rank the listed causes from most important (1) to least important (5). Write NC if the statement is not a cause at all.

1. Sidis is a public figure because:
   _____ a) he was a child wonder.
   _____ b) he gave lectures at Harvard when he was just a kid.
   _____ c) he appeared in the newspapers.
   _____ d) he was weird.
   _____ e) none of the above.

2. Sidis's right to privacy was violated because:
   _____ a) he had gone into seclusion and was no longer a public figure.
   _____ b) *The New Yorker* wrote a story about him.
   _____ c) the story in *The New Yorker* made fun of Sidis.
   _____ d) he had a famous father.
   _____ e) none of the above. (If you choose e, give a cause of your own.)

3. Sidis lost his case because:
   _____ a) the judge felt that *The New Yorker* was not acting out of malice.
   _____ b) Sidis was a public figure.
   _____ c) public figures do not have the same rights of privacy as other people.
   _____ d) he had a bad lawyer and this took place in 1937.
   _____ e) none of the above. (If you choose e, give a cause of your own.)

4. Sidis lived as a recluse and died in poverty because:
   _____ a) he did not have any money.
   _____ b) he did not have any friends.
   _____ c) his parents did not like him so they abandoned him.
   _____ d) he collected streetcar transfers and liked the Communist Party.
   _____ e) none of the above. (If you choose e, give a cause of your own.)

5. Sidis's unusual behavior was the result of:
   _____ a) an unusual family situation.
   _____ b) his father using him for experiments.
   _____ c) his coming from a long line of weirdos.
   _____ d) his not having a mother.
   _____ e) none of the above. (If you choose e, give a cause of your own.)

After you have ranked these causes, get together in a group to see whether you agree or disagree with each other. Spend some time discussing your disagreements. Then continue to the exercise below.

Exercise 3.8: More Essay Practice

Pick one of the topics below, and write a three-paragraph essay using cause and effect as the organizer.

1. A response to one of the reflection questions in Exercise 3.6
2. An explanation of one of the items and its cause in Exercise 3.7 and why you chose the cause you did
3. An explanation of how all of the causes of an item in Exercise 3.7 make sense—it is fun to pick an item that has particularly silly causes

Developing Your Ideas with Details

There is a saying: "don't sweat the small stuff." This is good advice for some things, such as worrying about ants at a picnic. But it is not necessarily good advice for writers. **Details,** or "the small stuff," are those little bits of information that can make the difference between clear, lively writing and thinking and outright confusion.

Details help to shape your thinking and bring clarity to complicated ideas. Consider the Sidis case for a minute. What details would you like to know about his childhood that might shed more light on why he ended up the way he did? For example, what was Mrs. Sidis like? What happened to Sidis while he was in the mental hospital? When you are evaluating cause and effect, details make a big difference. They help you find the "real" causal relationship underlying what appears on the surface.

Details also liven up writing. What is more interesting to read: "John drove a red car;" or, "John, just back from Jamaica and the world's most handsome guy, drove a lipstick red Miata?" You probably find the second sentence more interesting. Due to details, we know that John is handsome, travels, and likes hot red cars. Details bring writing to life and can help persuade the reader that what you say is, in fact, the "way it is."

Exercise 3.9: Detail Practice

Reach each of the following short scenarios, and quickly list at least five details that might be useful to know. There are no right or wrong answers; just rely on your own thinking.

Example

A teenager is having his locker searched by the assistant principal. The teenager is threatening to sue the school for invasion of privacy. A call has been made to his lawyer. What might the lawyer need to know? (privacy)

- *The teenager dresses outlandishly and is often singled out.*
- *The teenager in the past has associated with known drug users.*
- *The teenager has nothing in the locker but books and old gym clothes.*

1. You discover that your mail has been opened, and you suspect a close friend. Before you confront this person, what might you want to find out? (privacy)
2. You find out that a secret you told your health counselor is now a rumor in the gossip mill. What information would you need before you could "prove" a breach of confidentiality? (confidentiality)
3. A doctor has prescribed a new experimental medicine to treat your mother's asthma. She is afraid to question the doctor, but you are not. What might you want to know? (right to know)
4. Your application for a job as youth counselor at a camp for learning-disabled kids has been rejected. You are surprised by the rejection as you are disabled yourself and have two years' experience working with kids. What details would you want to know when talking to the director of the camp? (right to know)
5. Your boyfriend/girlfriend is very late for a date to celebrate your birthday. You have been sitting in a very nice restaurant for the past two hours. When your beloved appears (s)he is out of breath, wearing ratty old clothes, and looking disheveled. You are less than pleased and demand an explanation. What details would you want to know? (right to know)

By doing this exercise, you may have discovered that curious readers need to know detail and are not satisfied unless they do. Whatever you are writing, you need to satisfy your readers' needs by giving details and explanations.

Exercise 3.10: Revision Practice

Go back to the essay you wrote about the Sidis case. Underline the details, and note questions in the margin about things you would like to know more about. When you are finished, ask yourself these questions. Trade papers with a partner.

1. Read your work aloud. How does it sound? Does it make sense? Did you leave anything out?
2. Did you use paragraphs that flow logically? That is, does the first paragraph logically lead into the next one and so forth?
3. Have you used enough details? Can the reader get a mental picture of what you are writing about?
4. Are the causes and the effects described clearly?
5. How are the mechanics (spelling, punctuation, grammar)?

Trade papers with a partner. Read each other's work, and look specifically for the use of details. Now rewrite the essay based on what you have discovered about its strengths and weaknesses.

Essay Topic: Individuals and the Right to Privacy

Unlike the exercise you just completed, most of the time you will not be able to "make up" details to suit your essays. Instead you will have to use examples, either from your reading or from your own experience. Following are more case studies to give you practice in looking for the supporting details you need to develop your writing. These cases once again concern issues of privacy. What you are reading are summaries, but all of these events really happened, and the outcomes have shaped our legal system. Read the cases, and do the exercises that go with them. You should be looking especially for details that you can use to support your ideas about the cases.

CASE STUDY 3: (PART 1)

Judith Ann Harkey and Jeanne R. Harkey v. Michael Abate

On April 19, 1979, Judith Harkey and her daughter Jeanne went roller skating at a rink owned by Michael Abate. While they were there, they used the public restroom in the roller rink. Later Judith Harkey discovered that Mr. Abate had installed see-through panels in the restroom ceiling. This made it possible for him to spy secretly on women using the restroom, including the inside of the separately partitioned stalls. Harkey charged that Abate did spy on her in the restroom and that this was an invasion of her privacy. She sued for damages.

In his defense, Abate testified that he did not see Harkey or her daughter as they had said. However, he did admit that he had installed the panels in the roller-rink restroom. Harkey's lawyers countered that it is not necessary to prove that Abate actually saw Harkey in the restroom to prove a case for invasion of privacy.

Exercise 3.11: Reflection and Discussion

Think about the following questions, and discuss them in a group. You may want to write down your thoughts.

1. What is your general reaction to this case?
2. Do you think Harkey has a case? Why or why not?
3. What is the role of intent in this case? (**Intent** in law is important because it implies that the person thought about and planned to do something, which is different from acting out of impulse or on the spur of the moment.)
4. What would you want to have as evidence to build this case either for or against Abate?

CASE STUDY 3: (PART 2)
Harkey and Harkey v. Abate

The case was finally decided in the Michigan State Court of Appeals. Harkey's attorney argued that restroom spying could be characterized as an invasion of privacy. The definition of invasion of privacy is an "unreasonable intrusion upon the seclusion of another." The court needed to decide whether or not installing glass panels in the ceiling of the rest room constituted intrusion and was, in fact, an invasion of privacy. That decision would allow or disallow awarding damages to the Harkeys.

The court based its decision on a New Hampshire ruling in which a landlord had secretly installed listening devices in the bedrooms of his tenants' apartments. In that case, the tenants successfully argued that it did not matter whether or not the landlord actually used the listening devices; the very fact that they were there without the tenants' knowledge constituted an invasion of privacy. As a result, the court held that Harkey's right to privacy had been violated and that she was eligible for damages. She won.

One judge, J. H. Gills, disagreed with the ruling. In his written dissent, he cited other cases related to this same issue. Judge Gills believed that just having peepholes or listening devices installed was insufficient to cause harm. To prove invasion of privacy, there had to be proof that the devices were used.

Exercise 3.12: Cause-and-Effect Essay

Write a cause/effect essay about the reasons that the court decided as it did in this case. Use details from the case as well as your own experiences to support your ideas.

CASE STUDY 4:
Richard M. Ribas v. Joan Clark

In March of 1985, Richard Ribas and his wife were getting a divorce. As in many divorces, the couple agreed on a legally binding property settlement. During the property negotiations, the Ribases used Mr. Ribas's lawyer. Mrs. Ribas did not have any legal counsel of her own. After the settlement, Mrs. Ribas began to have second thoughts and contacted a lawyer. He reviewed the terms of the settlement and told her that she was going to have to pay some big taxes. He told her that the settlement was not fair as far as she was concerned. Mrs. Ribas was furious and phoned her ex-husband to tell him that she had retained a lawyer. They had a fight over the phone. Mrs. Ribas's attorney also called Mr. Ribas, and the conversation was equally as heated.

About an hour later, Mrs. Ribas was still stewing about her property settlement and her ex-husband. She walked into her friend Joan Clark's office and asked to use the phone to call her ex-husband. She also asked Joan to listen in on an extension phone, which she did. Mrs. Ribas then prompted her ex-husband to reveal the details of his phone conversation with her lawyer. She also got him to admit that he had prevented her from getting an attorney during the divorce and property-settlement proceedings. Mrs. Ribas went back to court. The conversation in Clark's office was used as evidence for fraud. Joan Clark was called as a witness, and her testimony was used as a way to support Mrs. Ribas's story.

Mr. Ribas sued Clark for invasion of privacy and intentional infliction of emotional distress. He charged that she had illegally eavesdropped on his private conversation with his ex-wife. His lawyer argued that Clark's testimony could not be used in court against him.

Exercise 3.13: Cause-and-Effect Essay

Is eavesdropping an invasion of privacy? Should the court have allowed Clark's testimony? What causes did the court have for not allowing Joan Clark's testimony to stand? Be sure to use details to support your case. Use your own experience, as well as the details in the case study itself, to support what you say.

The following case explores the issue of privacy from a variety of angles. Although this is not a recent event, it does bring up some real questions about the relationship between the media, a news event, and the personal lives of the people involved. As you read this case, try to decide which side of the argument you support. As you read, don't hesitate to "mark it up." This will help you organize your thinking and be aware of the biases that might exist in the summary of the case. Also think about cause and effect as you read. Examine your own value system as it determines your response to the reading.

CASE STUDY 5:
Time, Inc. v. James J. Hill

On September 9, 1952, three convicts escaped from the federal penitentiary in Lewisburg, Pennsylvania. After a few days on the run, during which they stole a car, shotguns, and ammunition, they came to Whitemarsh, a suburb of Philadelphia. There they invaded the home of James and Elizabeth Hill and their five children—three teenage daughters and twin boys. Despite the fact that the convicts held the Hills hostage, they behaved in a very civilized manner. In general, they were courteous and did not harm the Hills except to scare them to death. Ten days later, the convicts were captured in New York City on the Upper West Side. Two were killed in a gun battle with a police detective, who was also killed, and the third was captured.

Understandably, the incident received a good deal of press coverage. There was curiosity as to "what really went on" at the Hills' home at the hands of the convicts. The Hills were asked numerous times to give interviews to the press about their frightening experience. However, the Hills were not interested in publicity. Except for a few brief statements to the press, they refused to discuss the case. They felt the less said the better and took great pains to shield their children from the unwanted publicity. In fact, the Hills were so interested in maintaining their privacy that they refused all offers of payment for their story and eventually moved to Connecticut. Mr. Hill summarized his feelings in a written response to an interview request:

> For the best interests of our children, we have felt that it was best to avoid any course of action that might remind them of our experience in September, 1952. Following this policy, we have refused all radio, television, magazine, and newspaper offers connected with that experience.

As in most crimes of this kind, publicity and public interest gradually faded away and the Hills were left in peace. On February 28, 1955, *Life* magazine published a review of a recently opened Broadway play entitled *The Desperate Hours*. The review described the play as a "fictionalized" account of a "real-life crime." The article said that "Americans all over the country who read about the desperate ordeal of the James Hill family can see the story reenacted in Hayes' Broadway play based on the book *The Desperate Hours*." Photographs of the Hills' former home were used in the article, along with photos of scenes from the play. The play, although fiction, portrayed a family like the Hills being held hostage and submitting to unspeakable mental and emotional horrors at the hands of their captors. According to the article, the play was, in fact, a composite of a number of hostage crimes, not specifically the Hills' situation. The article presented a complicated pattern of truth and fiction, all portrayed between the covers of *Life* magazine.

The result for the Hills was not great. The review article immediately cast the Hills' private life into the public spotlight. Mr. and Mrs. Hill retained an attorney and sued *Life* magazine for invasion of privacy. The Hills won their suit initially, but it was appealed and finally taken all the way to the United States Supreme Court.

The Hill case presented to the Supreme Court a situation in which the court had to weigh an individual's right to privacy and the necessity of upholding the First Amendment guarantee of freedom of speech and the press. *Life* magazine is clearly in the business of reporting information to the public and represents freedom of the press. The Hills, on the other hand, represent an individual's right to privacy which is not guaranteed by the Constitution but is implied through an overlapping of other amendments.

In the end, the court decided that it could not be proven that *Life* magazine had knowingly or recklessly published falsities in the article, and therefore the case was overturned and the Hills lost. Six judges voted with the majority, and there were three dissenting judges.

Epilogue: Mrs. Hill eventually committed suicide. There was some speculation that her death was related to the constant publicity and the *Life* article.

Exercise 3.14: Reflection and Discussion

Think about the following questions, and discuss them in a group. You may want to write down your thoughts.

1. Do nonpublic people—everyday people like the Hills—have a right to a private life, even if they have been involved in a highly publicized situation? Why or why not?
2. Should children ever be forcibly subjected to public scrutiny? Why or why not?
3. Do artists have the right to use, without permission, the private lives of people as material for their work? Why or why not?
4. Should the press have any boundaries? In short, should there be limits to "freedom of the press and freedom of speech"? Why or why not?
5. At what level is the issue of personal privacy an ethical issue rather than a legal one? When does common sensitivity, compassion, and concern for the individuals in distress override the legal and power issues of the "right to know"?

Exercise 3.15: Cause-and-Effect Essay

After you have discussed the questions above, frame your own cause-and-effect thesis about the Hill case. Then, using either the cause or the effect essay structure, write an essay supporting that thesis. Again, be sure to use details from the story as well as any details from your own experience to support your case. Make sure you revise your work.

CHAPTER REVIEW
Putting It All Together

Select one of the topics below, and compose an essay that incorporates the writing skills you have acquired so far. Select the essay structure that you feel will work best: classification, comparison/contrast, or cause and effect.

General Writing Topics

1. Estelle Griswold was willing to put her reputation on the line, risk her job, and live with a criminal record to help guarantee the right to privacy for her patients. Is there some ideal that you are willing to risk everything for? What is it and why?

2. When might it be justified for a person to "lose" his or her right to privacy? Why?

3. What restrictions, if any, should be placed on our right to freedom of speech? Why?

4. If individuals have the "right to know," do they also have the responsibility to "find out," and, if so, what shape does that responsibility take? If not, is "ignorance truly bliss?"

5. When should the state intervene in a family situation that may involve abuse?

6. Should a lawyer or a priest ever violate the confidentiality of a person who has confided in her/him? Under what conditions?

7. Does the public have a right to know about politicians' private lives? Why or why not?

8. How much information should the federal government provide its citizens concerning how foreign aid is being spent? For example, if individuals in Congress are aware that our foreign aid is going to a country that is a major violator of human rights but is politically friendly to us, should the American people be informed and how should they respond?

Extra Writing Practice: Quotation Notations

Use the following quotations as you see fit. You may want to write short answers, use them as a freewriting exercise, or compose an essay.

1. **"We are what we repeatedly do. Excellence then is not an act but a habit."** Aristotle

    How accurate do you think Aristotle's claim is? If our behavior changes dramatically as we age, does who we are change as well?

    _____
    _____
    _____
    _____
    _____

2. **"The free state offers what a police state denies—the privacy of home, the dignity and peace of mind of the individual. The precious right to be let alone is violated once the police enter our conversations."** Chief Justice William O. Douglas

    What does this quotation suggest to you? What does Douglas mean by "once the police enter our conversations"?

    _____
    _____
    _____
    _____
    _____

CHAPTER Four

CIVIL RIGHTS AND THE CONSTITUTION

Chapter Goals

After studying this chapter, you will be able to:
- Understand methods of argumentation.
- Structure an argumentative essay in two ways.
- Predict opposing arguments and write counterarguments.
- Identify types of fallacies commonly used in arguments.
- Develop ideas and write argumentative essays.

Introduction

In this chapter, the focus is on issues surrounding civil rights. You will explore the different ways of defining civil rights and what they mean to you. Your written work will focus on learning how to write effective arguments. You will read some cases from the Supreme Court that are examples of very clear thinking and powerful writing —argumentation at its best.

In the United States, rights come in all sizes and shapes and are wrapped around every cause and ideal imaginable. **Rights** are at the heart of the Constitution. There are individual rights, family rights, student rights, and the right to vote, to pray, and to get an education.

Civil rights is a phrase that is commonly used. In the United States, civil rights are often protected or "granted" by federal law, and they are based in the Constitution. This is important because federal law overrides state law. For example, the Americans with Disabilities Act (ADA) governs all areas of discrimination based on disabilities. No state may create a law that changes these federal regulations.

Civil rights and legislation like ADA are based on the idea of **equality**, the belief that all Americans should have the same opportunity "for life, liberty, and the pursuit of happiness." Because of the way our system works, civil rights has, in most instances, come to mean fairness in the eyes of the law. Sometimes, these laws can be complicated and difficult to enforce. Many of them are dependent on civic and social behaviors that are embedded in our culture.

The concept of rights in general and civil rights in particular has changed the very nature and soul of a country that was founded on "freedom" and "equality" without including all its citizens in the definition of who was free and who was equal. Civil rights (protected by just a few amendments in the Constitution) is about redefining those definitions. Civil rights legislation has produced some of the most dramatic cases in our legal history. These cases provide some of the best examples of argumentation that can be found. This chapter will give you a chance to read written opinions of the Supreme Court justices and to think about the cases and issues that have been decided by the Supreme Court.

Rights: Are They Guaranteed?

The Constitution of the United States was ratified in 1789. Since then, it has been altered or "amended" 26 times. The first ten amendments, the **Bill of Rights**, were added all together, and the last amendment was added in 1967. As you can see, the Constitution and the rights granted within it are ever changing. Conflicting interests and desires are the force behind these changes, which reflect the social, cultural, and political issues of the times. For example, women acquired the right to vote in 1920, and the first state to allow women to vote was Wyoming. Today, most of us are horrified to think that more than 50 percent of the population (including both women and slaves) could not vote, and yet that was clearly an acceptable concept for most of the history of this country.

Much of the Constitution is open to interpretation. Some rights are given explicitly; other are implied (remember the work on privacy).

Exercise 4.1: The Rights "Quiz"

Below is a list of "rights" statements that focus on civil rights. Label those that you think are guaranteed by the Constitution "T" (true) and label "F" (false) those that you think are not. Guaranteed means rights protected specifically by the Constitution or protected by current interpretation of the Constitution.

The answers are at the end of the quiz, but because no one is grading this, try not to look at them until you have tried this on your own or with a partner.

1. _____ the right to own guns
2. _____ the right to peaceful demonstration
3. _____ the right to privacy
4. _____ the right to education
5. _____ the right to choose and practice your religion
6. _____ the right to trial by jury
7. _____ the right to defend yourself
8. _____ the right to marry whom you choose
9. _____ the right to vote at 18
10. _____ the right to birth control
11. _____ the right to assemble
12. _____ the right to freedom of the press
13. _____ the right to be a member of whatever organization you choose
14. _____ the right to do what you want in the privacy of your own home
15. _____ the right to refuse health care
16. _____ the right to die

Answers: 1, 5, 6, 9, 11, and 12 are the only rights guaranteed or currently interpreted as guaranteed by the Constitution of the United States. Others are rights that are protected by law but not guaranteed. There is a big difference between being guaranteed protection by the Constitution, which applies to everybody, and protection by the laws of a particular state. Why do you think this is true?

Exercise 4.2: Making Civil Rights Your Rights

Choose one or all of the following writing exercises.

1. Keeping in mind that only items 1, 5, 6, 9, 11, and 12 are actually guaranteed by the Constitution, choose one other item from the list, and write your opinion about why this right should be or should not be guaranteed by the Constitution. How would the guarantee of some of these other "rights" affect the quality of our lives? How would the guarantee be enforced legally?

2. Reflect on the entire list, and think about what those rights or lack of those rights means in the lives of people like you or your family and friends. Write about an experience that you have had or that you know about where you believe that a person's civil or individual rights have not been protected. Be careful to include enough background information so that your reader will be able to understand fully the situation.

3. Write a "Bill of Rights" for your family, and explain in two or three paragraphs at the end why you chose the rights you did.

Revise and Reflect

Exchange your writing with a partner and read the work aloud. Ask your partner the following questions:

1. Do you fully understand the ideas that are being written about?
2. Are there any portions that are unclear? If so, why?
3. What do you need to know more about?
4. What seems unnecessary to you, if anything?
5. Is the writing interesting? Does it have "fire"? (If a piece of writing has fire, it is fun to read. When a piece of writing has fire, the language leaps out and grabs the reader.) Help each other add words and phrases to make the piece come alive. Rewrite your piece to include the comments of your partner.

Essay Topic: Civil Rights: A Historical Perspective

Now that you have had a chance to think about rights in general terms and how the idea applies to you, you may want a little bit of a historical perspective.

The story of the Civil Rights Movement goes back to the 1954 Supreme Court decision of *Brown v. the Board of Education of Topeka Kansas*. This case was probably the most important Supreme Court decision of the 20th century. It established new rules to begin the desegregation of public schools. What is often not understood about *Brown v. the Board of Education of Topeka Kansas* is that the Court focused on segregation as an issue of equality. It did not say that segregation was inherently wrong. It stated that, "Segregation of children by race is taken to mean inferiority of blacks; it impedes motivation of black children to learn, therefore, segregated schools are inherently unequal." *Brown v. the Board of Education of Topeka Kansas* did not apply to businesses, private schools, or other institutions of society. This meant that private schools and private employers such as hotels, restaurants, and recreational facilities could continue to hire and fire and admit and exclude people on the basis of race.

Also, despite the Supreme Court ruling in *Brown...*, public institutions were only required to desegregate at "all deliberate speed." This translated into slow at best. As a result, in the 1950s, institutional racial discrimination was alive and well in the United States.

Soon the winds of change began to blow across the land. In 1955, the Montgomery, Alabama, bus boycott was sparked by Rosa Parks's decision to keep her seat on a public bus. In 1960, four black students from North Carolina Agriculture and Technology ordered lunch at an "all white" Woolworth's lunch counter in Greensboro, North Carolina. This action sparked a long sit-in. In 1962, James Meredith was not allowed to enroll at Mississippi State University because he was black. Meredith returned to school, escorted by federal marshals, and took his seat in class. By 1963, Martin Luther King had become the leader of the massive Civil Rights Movement. Finally, in June of 1963, John F. Kennedy announced that he would introduce a civil rights bill in the Congress. His announcement was in response to the long hard work of many citizens in the United States to promote civil rights in all aspects of American society.

Despite the popularity of the young President, sweeping civil rights legislation was not an "idea whose time had come" in the legislature. Rather, many leaders of the African American community doubted that either the Republicans or the Democrats could successfully pull off a civil rights bill that had teeth. To make matters worse Kennedy was killed, and Lyndon Johnson, as a brand new President, had to take up the fight where Kennedy left off. It was a very shaky start, but H.R. 7152 (the number of the civil rights bill in the House of Representatives) began its painful journey through the House.

Its major champion was a representative from the Bronx, New York, named Manny Cellar. The opposition was fierce and tough. The debate wore on and on. Cellar's biggest fear was that amendments would be added to the bill that would (a) prove to be so unacceptable that it would never pass or (b) weaken the bill to make it virtually powerless. As the process dragged on during the course of the week, 124 amendments were offered, debated, and voted on, but only 34 of them were accepted, making mostly technical changes. Finally, at the eleventh hour, the Honorable Howard Worth Smith, of Texas, delivered what he considered to be the fatal blow to the bill.

Judge Smith added the word sex, meaning "gender", to the list of categories that could not be discriminated against. Smith smugly thought that he could defeat the bill by including women as a protected group. A flustered Manny Cellar, who was something of a chauvinist himself, rose to speak out against the amendment but was cut off.

Neither Cellar nor Smith bargained on the power and speed of the reaction of the five women in the U.S. House of Representatives. They instantly rose in support of the bill. To most everyone's surprise, the amended bill was passed by a vote of 168-133.

Exercise 4.3: Essay Practice

Choose one of the following questions as a basis for writing an essay. This is an opportunity to practice the types of essays you worked on in previous chapters.

1. Do you think the kind of discrimination that James Meredith experienced at Mississippi State University is still evident in our country today? (compare/contrast)

2. Can you think of other forms of discrimination that continue today and do not seem to be held in check by the laws of this country? For example, are people still discriminated against on the basis of sex? (compare/contrast)
3. How would our lives be different if the Civil Rights Movement had not happened (cause/effect or compare/contrast)
4. How do you think racial discrimination was defined in the 1950s? Do you think that definition has changed? If not, why not? (compare/contrast)

Argumentation

Argumentation is a form of writing that involves forming reasons and drawing conclusions. Argumentation can be used to persuade readers to consider a different point of view, to change their minds, or to take a particular action. Sometimes, a persuasive piece is written to reinforce beliefs, but usually argumentation is aimed at persuading someone who does not agree with you. When writing argumentation it is important to keep your audience in mind at all times. This means anticipating audience response, arguing against audience bias, and using language carefully so as not to offend.

To **argue** means to state the reasons why a belief you hold is valid. If you wanted to argue back in 1954, for example, that African Americans should have equal opportunities in education, the first thing you would do is make a list of all the reasons why they should. You also would want to understand your opposition's point of view: the reasons people believe African Americans should not be allowed equal opportunities in education. It is only by knowing what your opposition will argue that you will be able to argue effectively.

Think, for a moment, about something closer to home. Remember back to the time you first wanted to go out on a real late-night date. Pretend you had very strict parents (or remember the ones you actually had) who seldom let you do anything you thought you should be able to do. How would you go about convincing them to let you stay out late on prom night?

You have a few options. You could say nothing, stay out all night, scare your parents to death, and worry about the consequences later, or you could directly ask to stay out until 4 A.M.—chances are your parents would simply say, "No!" A better approach would be to have a convincing argument that addresses their worries and calms their fears. In general, the structure of an argument is the same as for other kinds of essays. The big difference is that in an argument, you are guided by your audience and what the "opposition" thinks.

EATO in Action

One way to remember the four basic components of a general argument is with the acronym *EATO—Evidence, Audience, Thesis, Opposition*. If you do a good job on each of these things and you are well organized, your essay will be very strong.

EVIDENCE. Just as in the other essays you have written, if you make a claim you need to "prove it!" In this case, it would be wise to let your parents know that there will be a designated driver, a phone check-in at a certain time, and a chaperone (such as a friend's home where there will be parents) for the "after prom party."

AUDIENCE. In this case, you know your audience extremely well. Your style will be different when addressing a more "distant" audience.

THESIS. Remember; a **thesis** is the main claim that the writer is making. It is important to remember that a thesis is an opinion for which you are arguing. In this case, your claim is that it is very important for you to stay out until 4 A.M. after the high school prom.

OPPOSITION. You need to understand your opposition's point of view and anticipate their argument. To continue with the example, most parents live in real fear of the alcohol or drugs and driving combination. Late nights after a prom with no supervision have been the downfall of many young people. These fears must be taken into consideration if the argument for the late night party is to be successful.

Exercise 4.4: Essay Practice

1. Write a letter to your fictitious parents to convince them to let you stay out until 4 A.M. on prom night. Make sure you consider EATO in developing your argument. When you are finished, trade letters with a partner, and find out how convincing you were. Feel free to add additional evidence to your argument.

2. One area of discrimination that does not get as much focus as other areas is age. Many state and federal laws set age qualifications for all kinds of activities, such as driving a car, getting married, voting, and retiring. Yet, age is like sex or race—it is a characteristic that is beyond the person's control.

    The Supreme Court has considered the constitutionality of age discrimination. One issue has been the constitutionality of having a mandatory retirement age.

    Think about this issue, and decide whether you think forcing people to retire at a certain age is an example of age discrimination. Write a letter to your 70-year-old senator, arguing on one side or the other. Use EATO as a guide.

3. Arguments can be tough to write, especially if the thesis is somewhat indefensible. To get a flavor for this kind of writing, write another letter to the same senator arguing that there should be no minimum age for drinking and, further, that setting a minimum age is discriminatory.

Trade letters with a partner, and see if your argument is convincing. If not, how can it be improved?

Essay Topic: Gender and the Constitution

There are many laws and regulations designed to remedy the effects of past discrimination against women. In 1975, the Supreme Court upheld the U.S. naval law that gave female naval officers more time to qualify for promotions than male officers. The court argued that women are not given the same opportunities for professional service as men. Therefore, the navy could make gender distinctions to make up for past discrimination. However, many people continued to believe that a constitutional amendment was necessary to ensure gender equity as a legal right. The Equal Rights Amendment (ERA) was proposed with the idea that it would erase any gender biases in United States law. The ERA proposed very practical guarantees, such as equal pay for equal work and absolute nondiscriminatory practices in employment. However, the ERA would have ended *all* gender classifications, even those designed to remedy the effects of past discrimination against women.

The ERA was approved by Congress in 1972 and went to the states for **ratification** (approval by the State legislature). Thirty-eight states (three fourths of 50) are needed to ratify any amendment to the Constitution. This did not happen for the ERA. On June 30, 1982, time ran out for the amendment. As a result, some gender distinctions are still permitted in American law.

The entire ERA amendment read as follows:

Equality of rights under the law shall not be denied or abridged by the United States or by any State on account of sex.

The Congress shall have the power to enforce, by appropriate legislation, the provisions of this article.

This amendment shall take affect two years after the date of ratification.

Exercise 4.5: Outlining Arguments

Think about the ERA. Do you support it or not? Take a stand. Fold a piece of paper in half lengthwise. On the left-hand side, list all the reasons why you believe the ERA should (or should not) have been ratified. Get together in small groups to brainstorm reasons.

Next, think of the counterarguments (the opposition's point of view). For each of the reasons you have listed, write a counterargument in the right-hand column. In other words, what would the opposition say to "shoot down" each of your arguments? Once again, small groups might be helpful when listing opposition arguments.

Example: *The ERA should have been ratified.*

Why?	Why not?
The ERA would guarantee the rights of no gender discrimination. The Civil Rights Act is simply a law and can be more easily changed and amended than the Constitution.	The ERA would eliminate laws that made up for past discrimination
Men and women should be paid the same for the same work. The ERA would ensure this.	The ERA would eliminate gender differences that make sense: different bathrooms, women's or men's clubs, etc.
Men and women should have the same opportunities to pursue their professional and personal goals. The ERA would help do this.	The ERA would tie up the courts with countless lawsuits that would be required to enforce it.
The ERA would mean that women serve in combat, strengthening the military.	The ERA would mean that women serve in combat, weakening the military.
The ERA would protect all women from discrimination nationwide.	The ERA would take away local control over family issues such as divorce, child custody, etc.

Structuring an Argument

There are many ways to structure an argument. The two most basic and most often successful ways are outlined below.

Argument Structure A: Dealing with the Opposition Up Front

INTRODUCTION: The general background of the topic leading to the thesis.

THESIS: Your position—usually placed at the end of the introduction.

OPPOSITION SUMMARY: A general summary of the major points the opposition makes. These are presented as weak. Do not spend too much time on opposition arguments as you risk convincing your readers that the opposition argument is a good one.

EVIDENCE: The reasons (from the left-hand column of your outline) why you believe your thesis is valid. These will be arranged from least important to most important (you want to save your zingers for last). Spend time developing your reasons. You can't use the short answer approach; you need to be convincing. In a short three-to-four-page paper, each reason will have a solid paragraph that develops it. In a longer paper, reasons can go on for pages—in a book, for chapters.

CONCLUSION: Gets the reader back to your thesis and, as in all essay writing, no new evidence should be added.

Argument Structure B: Knocking Down the Opposition as You Go Along

INTRODUCTION: Same as Structure A.

THESIS: Same as Structure A.

EVIDENCE: This section alternates the opposition's positions with your evidence. Be sure to give the opposition very short time here—do not let the reader think this is what you are arguing. Identify the opposition points as points you disagree with (for example, "Although some people may say that X is true, in fact, Y . . . ").

   a. opposition knocked down; your point argued
   b. opposition knocked down; your point argued
   c. opposition knocked down; your point argued
   d. etc.

CONCLUSION: Same as Structure A

As you can see, the difference in structure is in the presentation of the evidence. In Structure A, the writer deals with the opposition arguments early on, dismisses them, and then goes on to present the counterargument. This form is especially useful when the opposition's arguments are not so strong that you need to tackle each one individually. Structure B should be used when the opposition's arguments are strong and you need to deflate each argument individually before presenting your own points of evidence. Look back over your ERA outline. Which structure do you think would fit the argument better? Why?

Exercise 4.6: Structuring Arguments

Sample Argument Strucure A

Read the argument below. Underline the thesis. Then double underline the topic sentence that is the main part of the evidence in each section, and label it "Reason 1," "Reason 2," "Reason 3," and so forth. Circle the opposition arguments.

The United States may guarantee its citizens freedom and democracy, but it does not ensure equality. Prejudice and discrimination are unfortunate and unavoidable in this country. Activists in the 1960s may have propelled the country to pass the Civil Rights Act of 1964 which addressed racial discrimination, but the act did nothing to deter the less visible but very substantial form of discrimination based on gender. The Equal Rights Amendment (ERA) to the Constitution, which would guarantee gender equality, was approved by Congress in 1972 and sent to the states for ratification. Unfortunately, the ERA failed. Thirty-eight states must ratify an amendment, and it was not ratified by enough states before the deadline of June 30, 1982. The failure of the ERA was a great tragedy for American women, and it is still a matter of great debate.

Opponents of the ERA have many criticisms, which range from uninformed to irresponsible. They argue, for instance, that the issue isn't important enough to justify a constitutional amendment. Indeed, it isn't even really an issue at all—women aren't really being discriminated against. Legislation like the ERA promotes a form of reverse discrimination and makes it more difficult to hire qualified people. The ERA had its chance and it failed; obviously, it didn't have any real, serious support among the people, or it would have passed.

First of all, anyone who believes that women aren't discriminated against should compare men's and women's salaries. For every dollar that a man earns, a woman earns only 59 cents. That means that women are paid only slightly more than half of what men are paid, a fact that is simply astounding. This is extremely unfair and discriminatory. If a man and a woman perform the same duties with the same skill and dedication, then they should also receive the same wage.

It is idealistic and misguided to believe that federal laws are enough to deter discrimination, and the Civil Rights Act of 1964 is an excellent example. The prejudice and discrimination that it targeted still continues 30 years later. The federal and state governments have had more than enough time to act on their own, and it is obvious that something more substantial is necessary. For real change to occur, the power and prestige of a constitutional amendment is necessary.

As for the charge that the ERA promotes reverse discrimination, the ERA simply states, "Equality of rights...shall not be denied or abridged by the United States or by any State on account of sex." Nowhere does the ERA suggest that women should be given preference over men. Instead, it seeks to assure that women will receive the same treatment as men.

The last argument against the ERA, that it didn't have enough support to pass, is the most legitimate but it too is flawed. The ERA only fell two states short of the number needed to ratify it, and many of the amendment's supporters maintain that the ERA simply wasn't given enough time to seek ratification. A ten-year limit for its ratification was imposed, a restriction that has been condemned as arbitrary and unfair. Indeed, it wasn't until quite recently that citizens in Mississippi remedied an embarrassing oversight and ratified the 14th Amendment abolishing slavery—more than 100 years after it was first sent to the states.

*Ten years after the fact, the need for gender equality still exists in the United States and the failure of the ERA remains unfortunate and devastating. The arguments in favor of the ERA are certainly more logical and valid than those against it, and they have not lost any of their urgency. This is a miscarriage of justice that must be addressed immediately. The ERA was not given a real chance to succeed, and that is an opportunity lost forever. Now, however, is the time to move forward and find other alternatives. Women in this country are a silent majority in need. Don't let another 100 years pass before **this** oversight is recognized and remedied.*

Sample Argument Structure B

Now look at this same essay rewritten to follow Structure B. Again, underline the thesis, double underline the topic sentences that show each point of evidence and label them "reasons," and circle the opposition arguments. Which structure do you think works better for this particular argument and why?

The United States may guarantee its citizens freedom and democracy, but it does not ensure equality. Prejudice and discrimination are unfortunate and unavoidable in this country. Activists in the 1960s may have propelled the country to pass the Civil Rights Act of 1964 which addressed racial discrimination, but it did nothing to deter the less visible but very substantial form of discrimination based on gender. The Equal Rights Amendment (ERA) to the Constitution, which would guarantee gender equality, was approved by Congress in 1972 and sent to the states for ratification. Unfortunately, the ERA failed. Thirty-eight states must ratify an amendment, and it was not ratified by enough states before the deadline of June 30, 1982. The failure of the ERA was a great tragedy for American women, and it is still a matter of great debate.

Opponents of the ERA have many criticisms, which range from uninformed to irresponsible. For instance, there are those who claim that gender discrimination isn't even really an issue at all—it isn't really taking place. Anyone who believes that women aren't discriminated against should compare men's and women's salaries. For every dollar that a man earns, a woman earns only 59 cents. That means that women are paid only slightly more than half of what men are paid, a fact that is simply astounding. This is extremely unfair and discriminatory. If a man and a woman perform the same duties with the same skill and dedication, then they should also receive the same wage.

According to some people, the issue of gender discrimination isn't important enough to justify a constitutional amendment. However, it is idealistic and misguided to believe that federal laws are enough to prevent discrimination, and the Civil Rights Act of 1964 is an excellent example of this. The prejudice and discrimination that it targeted still continues 30 years later. The federal and state governments have had more than enough time to act on their own, and it is obvious that something more substantial is necessary. For real change to occur, the power and prestige of a constitutional amendment is necessary.

As for the charge that legislation like the ERA promotes a form of reverse discrimination and makes it more difficult to hire qualified people—this is simply untrue. The ERA merely states, "Equality of rights . . . shall not be denied or abridged by the United States or by any State on account of sex." Nowhere does the ERA suggest that women should be given preference over men. Instead, it seeks to assume that women will receive the same treatment as men.

The last argument against the ERA, that it had its chance and it failed, is the most legitimate, but it too is flawed. It is too simple to dismiss the ERA because, obviously, it didn't have any real, serious support among the people or it would have passed. The ERA only fell two states short of the number needed to ratify it, and many of the amendment's supporters maintain that the ERA simply wasn't given enough time to seek ratification. A ten-year limit for its ratification was imposed, a restriction that has been condemned as arbitrary and unfair. Indeed, it wasn't until quite recently that citizens in Mississippi remedied an embarrassing oversight and ratified the 14th Amendment abolishing slavery—more than 100 years after it was first sent to the states.

*Ten years after the fact, the need for gender equality still exists in the United States, and the failure of the ERA remains unfortunate and devastating. The arguments in favor of the ERA are certainly more logical and valid than those against it, and they have not lost any of their urgency. This is a miscarriage of justice that must be addressed immediately. The ERA was not given a real chance to succeed, and that is an opportunity lost forever. However, now is the time to move forward and find other alternatives: Women in this country are a silent majority in need; don't let another 100 years pass before **this** oversight is recognized and remedied.*

Exercise 4.7: Essay Practice

Write an essay that supports or opposes the ERA. Choose one of the argument structures above, and argue your case carefully and clearly. When you finish the essay, exchange it with a partner, and go through the revision process.

Have your partner read your essay, checking it against the list of questions below.

1. Does the essay address all the points the writer wanted to make? (If you are not sure, discuss it.)
2. Is the information presented clearly?
3. Are you convinced of the argument?
4. If you held the opposing view, would you be convinced?
5. Could you add anything to the argument to make the writer's case stronger?
6. Are the examples convincing?

Extended Analogies

In Chapter Two, you practiced writing analogies for compare/contrast essays. In everyday conversation you use analogies to spice up a description or to show understanding of a friend's situation because you experienced something similar. Analogies can also be extended. As you already know, an analogy is a powerful argumentative tool. It can pull a reader (or a listener) into a particular point of view because the point of view seems to be so clear in the analogy. Through the power of the analogy, the reader's focus is drawn away from questioning the validity of the position.

An **extended analogy** is a simple comparison developed into a longer comparison. Many poems are extended analogies. Let's take a look at an example of an extended analogy. Suppose someone feels that their rights as a white male are being violated by an **affirmative action** program that seeks to increase the number of minorities enrolled in a medical school. The person uses the following analogy: "Refusing me entry into medical school because I'm white and a male is like refusing to let nonwhites eat in "all white" establishments. Both are examples of discrimination."

At first glance, this seems a sensible analogy: one could argue that both examples do show discrimination. But look more closely at the analogy. What are the similarities? That two people, one nonwhite and one white, are denied entrance to something. But there are some major differences between the two parts of this analogy. Here's a list:

1. Going to medical school is certainly not the same as eating in a restaurant. There may be many reasons that a person is not accepted in school, and the reason that he is white and male would be awfully hard to prove. Admissions requirements are varied. There may be parts of his record that are too weak for admittance. There are complex admissions practices such as the "preferential" treatment for many candidates, including children of alumni, good athletes, or even sometimes, wealthy candidates. Affirmative action is only one part of the whole picture. Unlike applying to graduate school, going into a restaurant is not something one must compete for: there are no entry requirements.

2. Going to medical school is not a right; it is something many people want to do but not all can. Most of us would agree that although it is not protected specifically by the Constitution, we feel we have a right to go where we choose to go unless there is a legitimate reason for some prohibition.

3. No laws exist guaranteeing a person's right to attend medical school. However, a law does exist guaranteeing a person's right not to be excluded from a public place because of race.

4. There are a limited number of slots open for medical students. The medical school may want to graduate doctors of various backgrounds to reflect the various populations that need medical care. This means admitting people of varying backgrounds. Restaurants are not preparing people for service in diverse communities; they are serving food. In fact, restaurants often depend on serving as many people as possible, and forbidding one type of population to receive their services violates a social need.

The list of differences could go on. Would another analogy make the point better? Instead of using a restaurant, he might use something that is a little more closely related to his topic: "Refusing me entry into medical school because I am white and male is like refusing a nonwhite woman entry into the local Rotary Club." Here, although medical school and a club are apparently different, there are some basic, major similarities that are more to the point.

1. Both places give a person access to helping other people. A medical student becomes a doctor who, presumably, will go out and do good for people. A Rotarian spends time raising money for good causes.
2. There are some requirements for entry into each position.
3. Entry is not guaranteed to all but must be applied for.
4. The rejection of a qualified nonwhite woman from an organization such as the Rotary, simply because of race and gender, is much closer to the situation the medical-school candidate wants to argue.
5. There is the element of outrage. The reader is likely to be outraged by the exclusion of the nonwhite woman from the Rotary, and the writer hopes that outrage extends to his situation as well.

Exercise 4.8: Reflection and Discussion

You have practiced writing analogies in Chapter Two, and you know that analogies can be very powerful tools in writing. Below you will find a list of civil rights-related topics for which you can create analogies. Finish each of the statements with an appropriate analogy. Be sure to test the analogy and to rewrite it if it doesn't work.

1. Sending Japanese Americans to detention camps during World War II was like...
2. Denying migrant workers health benefits is like...
3. Becoming an American citizen is like...
4. Freedom of the press is like...
5. Making public the names of all sex offenders in a given neighborhood is like...

Share your analogies with the class or with a small group. Any of these analogies could be extended and used effectively in an argument. As you go through this chapter, keep this exercise in mind and try to weave relevant analogies into your writing.

CASE STUDY 1:

Fred Toyosaburo Korematsu v. United States

"To oversee a government is a cautious balancing act." The Supreme Court relies upon a "balancing act" when making judgments between individual freedom and the public interest. During wartime, the Court's balance often weighs in the direction of restricting individual freedom.

During World War II, after the Japanese bombed Pearl Harbor, the country was swept with a fear of international attack. On February 2, 1942, under the War and National Emergency power of the Congress and the President,

Franklin Roosevelt, issued Executive Order 9066. The order read in part, "...all persons of Japanese ancestry, including citizens whose loyalty is not questioned" were to be excluded from certain areas of the West Coast. Within a week, 120,000 Japanese Americans were taken from their homes, transported to centrally located "assembly areas," and "relocated" to one of ten internment camps. The camps were administered by the War Relocation Authority and were located in Arizona, Arkansas, Wyoming, Colorado, Utah, and California. Many of these people had family members serving in the U.S. armed forces.

The purpose of this act was to prevent spying and sabotage of the United States West Coast war effort. It was based on the logic that there was no quick way to identify Japanese people who continued to be loyal to Japan. (A note of irony is that Hawaii, with the largest Japanese American population in the nation and the site of Pearl Harbor, was exempt from the "relocation" order.)

Fred Toyosaburo Korematsu was born in California of parents who had immigrated to this country from Japan. He was a citizen of the United States and a resident of the state of California. Korematsu refused to leave his home and report to an assembly center. His reason was that he was a U.S. citizen and he had done nothing wrong.

Korematsu was arrested and convicted of remaining in a military area from which persons of Japanese ancestry had been ordered excluded. He was sentenced to five years' imprisonment but was immediately paroled. Korematsu turned to the United States court system to challenge the constitutionality of Executive Order 9066. The case was argued October 11 and 12, 1944, in front of the Supreme Court of the United States and decided December 18, 1944. He lost.

Supreme Court Justice Hugo Black wrote the majority opinion. Justice Black began his opinion with this statement:

> It should be noted, to begin with, that all legal restrictions which curtail the civil rights of a single racial group are immediately suspect. That is not to say that all such restrictions are unconstitutional. It is to say that courts must subject them to the most rigid scrutiny.

Black went on to argue that there are times when the safety or well being of the public may justify restricting the civil rights of a single racial group. While racial hostility is never a valid reason for such restrictions, excluding people of Japanese descent from certain areas of California to ensure national security in times of national emergency was well within the bounds of the war power of the Congress and the President. Justice Black noted that at least 5,000 U.S. citizens of Japanese ancestry refused to swear loyalty to the United States and to renounce their loyalty to the Japanese emperor. He further noted that there were several thousand individuals who requested to be returned to Japan. Black concluded that exclusion and relocation of Japanese Americans was not based on racial antagonism but rather on national security.

Justice Roberts dissented. He began his argument as follows:

> I dissent because I think the indisputable facts exhibit a clear violation of constitutional rights. This is not a case of temporary exclusion of a citizen from an area for his own safety or that of the community, nor a case of offering him an opportunity to go temporarily out of an area where his

presence might cause danger to himself or to his fellows. On the contrary, it is the case of convicting a citizen as a punishment for not submitting to imprisonment in a concentration camp, based on his ancestry, and solely because of his ancestry, without evidence or inquiry concerning his loyalty …toward the United States.

Justice Murphy also dissented. He began his argument with the following statement:

This exclusion of 'all persons of Japanese ancestry, both alien and non-alien,' from the Pacific Coast area on a plea of military necessity in the absence of Martial Law ought not be approved. Such exclusion goes over 'the very brink of Constitutional power' and falls into the ugly abyss of racism.

Although Justice Murphy agreed that the judgment of the military and the executive branch should not be overruled lightly, he argued that individuals should not be deprived of their constitutional rights on the strength of a military claim that has neither substance or support. The stated purpose of the executive order was to prevent sabotage and spying. However, assuming that all people of Japanese ancestry would be potential saboteurs or spies and therefore should be removed from their homes and imprisoned is not reasonable. There is no reliable evidence to show that all persons of Japanese descent are generally disloyal or have participated in actions that threaten the security of the nation.

Justice Murphy further cited testimony of the commanding general as an indication of racial prejudice.

I don't want any of them (persons of Japanese ancestry) here. They are a dangerous element. There is no way to determine their loyalty….The danger of the Japanese was, and is now . . . espionage and sabotage. It makes no difference whether he is an American citizen, he is still Japanese….But we must worry about Japanese all the time until he is wiped off the map.

Murphy concluded his argument as follows:

I dissent, therefore, from this legalization of racism. Racial discrimination in any form and in any degree has no justifiable part whatever in our democratic way of life. It is unattractive in any setting but it is utterly revolting among a free people who have embraced the principles set forth in the Constitution of the United States. All residents of this nation are kin in some way by blood or culture to a foreign land. Yet they are primarily and necessarily a part of the new and distinct civilization of the United States. They must accordingly be treated at all times as the heirs of the American experiment and as entitled to all the rights and freedoms guaranteed by the Constitution.

Epilogue: On August 10, 1988, President Regan signed into law a bill that gave an apology and paid reparations to Japanese Americans who were put into internment camps during World War II. Regan declared:

It's not for us today to pass judgment upon those who may have made mistakes while engaged in that great struggle. Yet, we must recognize that the internment of Japanese Americans was just that—a mistake… What is important in this bill has less to do with property than with honor, for here we admit a wrong.

Exercise 4.9: Reflection and Discussion

The beginning of this chapter discussed "guaranteed" rights. However, because we live under a system where different interests are in power at different times, when it comes to matters of the law, nothing is guaranteed.

In the case of the Japanese internment camps, racism played a significant role. What are other situations in society where similar legal decisions/situations have occurred?

Think about the following questions and discuss them in a group. You may want to write down your thoughts.

1. How do isms affect our legal system? (Refer back to Chapter Two if necessary.)
2. What do we do about isms in our legal system?
3. What implications does the Korematsu case have for U.S. citizens in times of war or other national emergencies?
4. What standards should be created to provide a good balance between public safety and personal freedom?
5. Which justice's argument made the most sense to you and why?

Exercise 4.10: Essay Practice

After thinking about these questions, take a position that you could argue. For example, you might decide to expand on the argument of one of the Supreme Court justices or on the answer to one of the discussion questions. Write an argumentative essay using the techniques you have learned in this chapter. Try to make your writing as interesting as possible. This is a good opportunity to practice analogies. Make sure you go through the revision process.

Argumentative Context

You know from your own experience that what *you* mean by a word is not necessarily what someone else means. So too, meanings of words change and shift when the situation, or **context**, shifts. Think, for example, of the word *worm*. In an industrial context, a worm is part of a machine that bores into the earth. In *Star Trek*, worm is short for worm hole and means "a tunnel in space that gives quick access to different parts of the universe." In a medical context, worm means "parasite." As an insult, being called a worm implies that the person is not very brave or trustworthy.

Another example is the word *spell*. To a teacher, spell means "to place the correct letters in the correct order." To a magician, a spell is a magical formula. In some parts of our country, being taken with a spell means that a person has taken sick.

Shifting context is a way to open yourself to different ideas. Unlike changing context, a shift in context does not change the entire meaning of a word or concept. Rather, it changes the interpretation, based on the viewpoints of different people.

Exercise 4.11: Shifting Context

Write a paragraph defining *civil rights* in the context of two of the groups listed below. Pick categories that in your mind are dissimilar.

African Americans
Handicapped, or
  physically challenged, people
Native Americans
Single-Parent Families
Arab Americans
White Males
Yourself, Your Family

Exchange your paragraph with a partner, and answer the following questions:

1. Does the term *civil rights* shift or change as the context changes?
2. If the term does not change, why do you suppose that is?
3. What have you discovered about the term *civil rights* from your partner's paper?
4. Do you disagree with any of the writer's points? Write a short paragraph at the bottom of your partner's paper explaining your disagreement.
5. What do your definitions say about your assumptions about a particular group?

Shifting contexts is a good habit to get into, especially when you are dealing with argumentation. A context shift broadens your views about a situation. It also allows you to see more clearly the opposition's point of view and to see an issue from many angles. Most issues are not cut and dried; rather, they are fairly complex. Being able to shift contexts around an issue can help you see the complexities of the issue before you start arguing it.

Exercise 4.12: Essay Practice

Pick one of the contexts listed in Exercise 4.11 and write an argumentative essay. For example, you might argue that handicapped people ought to have equal access to all public and private buildings. Choose an argumentative structure, and prepare carefully before you write. When you are finished, switch papers with a partner, evaluate each others' work, and make revision suggestions.

Fallacies in Argument

A chapter about writing arguments and essays would not be complete without a final word on fallacies. **Fallacies** is a fancy word that pretty much means bad or faulty claims. Fallacies, or unsound arguments, are particularly tricky because they often seem to make sense. In many cases they appeal to our emotions and prejudices and often support ideas that we want to believe are true. It is important for you as a writer and reader to understand what fallacies are and to be able to spot them in your own writing and thinking as well as in that of others.

Logical fallacies are junk—bad arguments that often sound good but do not hold up upon close examination. Many logical fallacies are thrown our way in today's popular culture—in arguments, advertisements, newspaper articles, books, and so forth.

Following is an example of an argument that contains quite a few fallacies. See if you can spot the fallacies—weak arguments, illogical claims, and things that just don't seem right. Circle or underline them. Make notations in the margins, if you wish.

Voting Is Not Child's Play
by Myles Freer

Recently, in the name of so-called "Children's Rights," I read a proposal by Mr. Ed Huitema, calling for children (age 13 and above) to have the right to vote in public elections! It's not so surprising that such a moronic proposal would come from a slow wit like Huitema. He is a constant complainer. To him I say, "America—Love it or Leave it!"

Why not give children the right to vote? Well for starters, children are (not too surprisingly) child-like. I think we can all agree that opening up the vote to even more child-like voters (joining Mr. Huitema that is), would be a mistake. I wonder what proof Mr. Huitema could give us that giving children the right to vote won't wreak havoc on the very fabric of our great society? Look at the problems around us. We know that kids are shooting each other in the schools and in the streets. The news and the statistics prove it. They have guns; let's not also give them the vote.

Types of Fallacies

Fallacies tend to fall into categories. Following is an analysis of the argument, pointing out the types of fallacies used.

Name calling is an example of a fallacy called *ad hominem*. This is Latin for "against the person." Insults are not arguments (it doesn't matter if Mr. Huitema is a "slow wit" or not; he may have a good point).

"America—Love it or Leave it" is an example of the **either/or** or **false dilemma** fallacy. This is your claim that there are only two sides to an issue—and nothing in between (or beyond). Why just "Love" or "Leave"? A democracy is based on an exchange of ideas—debate, reflection, change. The "Love it or Leave it" perspective is in many ways antidemocratic (and some would say anti-American). "You are either for us or against us" is another common example of this. What does it mean to be "for" someone? In what circumstances? To what degree?

Don't give children the right to vote because "children are child-like" is an example of **begging the question**. This is your use of your conclusion as a reason to support the conclusion. Children are by *definition* child-like, so what the writer is saying is "children are children." So what? What is it about children that *means* they should not vote? The statement doesn't answer this question.

"What proof can Mr. Huitema give us...." This fallacy is called **appeal to ignorance**. The fact that Mr. Huitema cannot prove something does not mean that the opposite is true. I cannot prove that it won't rain tomorrow; this does not mean that it will.

"We know that kids are shooting each other..." This fallacy has the fancy name of **irrelevant thesis**. The writer is not arguing about the right of kids to vote; he is claiming that kids shoot each other and then trying to tie it to voting. In other words, he is arguing about one subject when he is really trying to make a point about another. He does not tie in a connection for us.

The key to discovering fallacies is to get used to watching for them as a matter of habit. You might be surprised how often they turn up.

Exercise 4.13: Fallacy Practice

Following is a list of different fallacies and an example of each one. In parentheses is an explanation about why each example fits that category. For each type of fallacy, write two additional examples. When doing this, think about situations where you may have heard or read someone use some questionable reasoning. Controversial subjects usually are a hotbed for fallacies. If you find this exercise difficult, you may wish to work with a partner.

1. **EITHER/OR** *Either we will build this new sports complex, or this town will become a ghost town full of the unemployed.*
   (There is usually more than one choice in any given situation. There may be another way the town can bring in revenue and jobs.)

   a) _____

   b) _____

2. **APPEAL TO IGNORANCE** *UFO's exist! No one has proved that they don't.*
   (Just because something hasn't been disproved doesn't mean it is true.)

   a) _____

   b) _____

3. **IRRELEVANT THESIS** *We mustn't let the town change property taxes. Remember last year when they screwed up the schedule for recycling.*
   (Even though the town screwed up one thing doesn't mean it will screw up a different thing. The two are not necessarily connected.)

   a) _____

   b) _____

4. **BEGGING THE QUESTION** *Rude rock and rap lyrics should have a warning label because they are crude and harsh.*
   (To be "crude and harsh" is to be rude. All this claim is really saying is "Rude rock and rap lyrics are rude." It isn't saying why being rude should result in a warning label.)

   a) _____

   b) _____

Exercise 4.14: More Fallacy Practice

1. Practice doing it the wrong way. Write a short essay using at least three types of fallacies. Pick your own topic or use one of the thesis statements below:

   The Equal Rights Amendment was a bad (or good) idea.

   There should (or should not) be a curfew for teenagers living in cities.

   Private clubs, where members apply and pay a fee to join, should (or should not) be able to select members on the basis of race and/or gender.

   Share your writing with a partner and see if he or she spots all of the fallacies.

2. After writing your essay, rewrite it replacing the fallacies with good reasons.

Essay Topic: Freedom of Speech

Following are more cases to stimulate more thinking and writing. Each of these cases deals with aspects of individual and civil rights. This will give you plenty of opportunity to practice argumentative essay writing.

CASE STUDY 2:
Bethel School District No. 403 v. Framer

In the spring of 1983, Bethel High School in Tacoma, Washington, was in search of a student vice president. The president of the class, Matthew Framer, nominated his friend for the job. In a rather typical adolescent move, Matthew's nominating speech was filled with sexual analogies and overtones. The speech was greeted with "hoots and hollers," hand gestures, and generally raucous behavior from the 600-member student audience.

The morning after the speech, the assistant principal called Framer into her office and told him that his speech had been in violation of school rules. Framer was given copies of five letters from teachers describing his behavior in the assembly. He was given a chance to explain himself, and he admitted to using sexual suggestion in his speech. The school officials responded by suspending Matthew for three days and not allowing him to be chosen as a commencement speaker.

Matthew sued the school district, saying that his right of free speech had been violated. The school appealed using the following arguments: 1) The speech was disruptive; 2) The school has the right to discipline a student who makes "indecent" remarks; 3) The school has a right to discipline behavior that is considered objectionable when it occurs at a school-related function.

Exercise 4.15: Argumentative Essay

Write an opinion piece taking a side for or against Framer. Practice arguing against or for specific points.

Questions to consider:
1. How do you think the courts should decide this case?
2. What do you see to be the long range effects of either a "pro" or "con" decision?
3. How far do the rights of school administrators go in controlling the content and style of students' speech and writing?

DON'T READ ANY FURTHER UNTIL YOU HAVE WRITTEN YOUR ESSAY.

The Supreme Court decided in favor of the school district because "The First Amendment guarantees wide freedom in matters of adult public discourse....The constitutional rights of students in public school are not automatically coextensive with the rights of adults in other settings." In other words, students do not have adult rights according to this decision. The judges did not see the school's disciplinary action as a violation of free speech. They argued that Framer was being punished for disrupting the assembly. Justices Marshall and Stevens dissented. They argued that the school district failed to prove that Framer's speech was disruptive. Although both judges agreed that school faculty must regulate content and style of student speeches, they must also give fair notice of the punishment. In other words, they must let students know ahead of time what the consequences of their actions will be.

Exercise 4.16: Argumentative Essay

Write a short essay arguing for or against the Supreme Court's decision. Be sure you understand both sides of the case before you argue your own.

CASE STUDY 3:

Freedom to Cheer

From the days of the Roman half-time shows of lions eating Christians, crowds have loved to cheer and jeer at sporting events. It seems that human nature cannot let a contest go by on an athletic field without noise and comment. But what happens when that noise and comment becomes offensive to some? What happens to "freedom of expression" then?

The Detroit Tigers and the ACLU (American Civil Liberties Union) became involved in a dispute over the Tigers' cheering fans. The fans have a reputation of poor behavior in the stands and have been known to throw "beach balls, bottles, nuts, bolts and golf balls" onto the field. The management of the Tigers had been trying to find a way to slow down and control the "bleacher creatures," those people who sat in the cheap seats and sang obscene words to the tune of beer commercials. The management closed the bleachers and posted signs saying "No chanting of any kind."

The ACLU saw this as a violation of free speech and the rights of fans to cheer for the home team. The management changed the sign to "No obscene chanting of any kind." This time the ACLU questioned the management's right to decide what was obscene. The management of the Tigers argued that fans who paid money to see the game had a right to privacy. In this case, privacy translates into being left alone to watch the game and not being subjected to crowds of people chanting songs with foul lyrics.

The ACLU argued that the right of freedom of speech and the suppression of censorship was more important than being able to watch the game in relative peace.

Exercise 4.17: Argumentative Essay

Do you agree with the team management or the ACLU? Write an essay presenting your argument. Ideas to consider:

1. What are people's expectations when they go to a sporting event? Does it depend on the event? Does it depend on whether the event is free or costs money? Would the same rules apply at a hockey game? At a local public school soccer match?

2. Is there a difference between speech on private property and public property?

CHAPTER REVIEW
Putting It All Together

Select one of the topics below and compose an essay. Use everything you have learned from this book.

General Writing Topics

1. What does "life, liberty and the pursuit of happiness" mean?
2. Is there an ism with which you align yourself? What is it and why?
3. Are there ever times or conditions under which a government has a right to limit the civil rights of any or all of its citizens?
4. What is the state of civil rights in this country today? What is working? What still needs to be addressed?
5. What is the best method to bring about change in this country regarding civil rights? Legislation? Amendments to the Constitution? Protests? Others?
6. Some people have argued that certain groups are demanding "special rights" instead of civil rights. What do you think of this claim?
7. Should institutions (public and private) develop practices (such as hiring) that give special consideration to a group that has been discriminated against in the past? If so, what should they do and why? If not, why not?

Extra Writing Practice: Quotation Notations

This is the final set of these little words of wisdom. We hope you have enjoyed writing and thinking about them. Select from the following list, and use the quotation to write one of the types of essays you have studied.

1. "In a democracy, no man has the right to be ignorant about the basic institutions under which he lives. He may have other rights but he does not have this one." Edgar Dale

   Is anyone responsible for informing citizens of their rights? If so, who? Why? If not, why not?

2. "There are two kinds of freedoms: the false where a man is free to do what he likes; the true where a man is free to do what he ought." Charles Kingsley

   How does Kingsley's claim fit in with the right to pursue happiness?

3. "Predicting rain doesn't count, building arks does." The Noah Principle

   What does this statement mean to you?

4. "What the people want is very simple. They want an America as good as its promise." Barbara Jordan

   What has "America" promised? Can we agree on what the promises are? What would it take to live up to these promises? Is it possible or worth striving for? Why or why not?

ANSWER KEY

Chapter 2

ANSWERS TO EXERCISE 2.4

1. T
2. A/Rewrite: Families are the basis of our society.
3. T
4. A/Rewrite: Children should obey their parents.
5. T
6. F/Possible rewrite: Blood does not a sibling make.

ANSWERS TO EXERCISE 2.5

Dogs Are Family Members Too

Introduction: The other day while I was visiting a friend of mine, she told me her dog had died. Feeling very sad, she said it was like losing a member of the family. "But Betty," I insisted, "it's not like losing a member of the family; you did lose a member of your family." Betty wasn't so sure.

I know that many people have many different definitions of what makes up a family. In some cultures families are not just blood relatives or adopted children, but the whole village. In other cultures families are seen as only parents and children. *Thesis:* However, I say that when a family has a dog, that dog is a member of the family.

Families are social units whose members care about each other. Family members take care of each other. Family members learn from each other. They have good times and bad times, but they usually tough it out. In our culture the immediate family often lives together. *Evidence 1:* <u>Dogs do all these things. Dogs certainly care about the family, protect the family, enjoy the family, and bring pleasure to the family. Dogs live with the family.</u>

Some people would say "Dogs don't teach us anything" or "Dogs don't understand what's going on so they can't be full members of the family" or "Only people can be members of families." I disagree. <u>Dogs remind us to have fun, to not take life so seriously.</u> This is an important thing to learn. And while it's true that dogs don't understand what is going on in the family, children often do not either. Children are certainly family members. Finally, why limit our vision of family to creatures just like ourselves? <u>Everyone in a family contributes in a unique way. While dogs are different they still do many of the things that other members do—they just do it with a twist.</u>

— Evidence 2

— Evidence 3

Conclusion { Betty was very sad that her family lost their dog. I was sad too that they had lost a member who protected them, made them laugh, challenged them, loved them and was loved by them. In other words, they lost a family member because dogs are family members too.

Chapter 3

ANSWERS TO EXERCISE 3.3

1. Causes that drove Buxton and Griswold:
   a. Belief that all people should have equal access to birth control
   b. Belief that a person's medical records are private/confidential
   c. Belief that only though civil disobediance could the law be changed
2. Moral issues:
   a. All people should have equal opportunity.
   b. Privacy is a personal right.
   c. People have the right to challenge laws they disagree with.
3. Which is the most important cause?
   This is a matter of personal opinion.
4. What is the overall effect of the Griswold case?
   A change in the law.